Angela Bowie

FREE
SPIRIT

MUSHROOM BOOKS

EDITED BY Don Short

ISBN: 0 907 39403 5
Published by Mushroom Publishing Ltd,
102 Gloucester Place, London W1
Printed and bound by Purnell

DEDICATION

I dedicate this book to my son Zowie, with love and affection.

IF I AM
TO BE
REMEMBERED
AT ALL
LET ME BE
REMEMBERED
AS I AM,
A FREE
SPIRIT

—Angela Bowie
APRIL 2, 1980

I have come upon a thought of heaven,
open, empty paper must promise paradise,
but why write beauty so others may admire your vision,
is not the inner knowledge that you saw the truth
more blessed than the appreciation of others to this art,
an empty page holds promises of joy and ecstasy,
no written word can be superior to the promise,
it may be great and sweet and heavenly in its
inspiration but there is no assurance,
that the emptiness of space will acknowledge
perfection more poignantly.
These words describe my thought,
let them not be cursed for being written,
please let the idea serve to rise above my ugly ink imprints and satisfy your soul,
whose pleasure not admiration I cherish.

PREFACE

The conventional concept of marriage would not have suited my style. Not in 1970. Nor in David Bowie's intrepid new world.

I was a butterfly. And a bisexual one too.

Expelled from a girl's college for having an illicit affair, I was prepared to become David's wife on a mutual understanding that our marriage would be governed by contemporary codes.

We vowed that infidelity would never threaten our marriage.

We vowed that we would never give way to jealousy or possessiveness.

We vowed that we would never harbour secrets from one another.

We vowed that we would remain together forever and that no one would infringe our commitment.

Idealistic maybe, but essentially idyllic.

We were convinced we could make our unique pact work, because we had removed the one obstacle that had plagued human relationships for centuries: suspicion.

"Suspicion is the one element that kills a marriage," I said to David, "let us always be totally frank and honest with one another."

David said, "Whatever happens, you will always be my love. The only person who will still figure in my life when everyone else has gone."

Blatantly, we boasted of our marriage and of its concept to the world.

Society reeled, paused to examine our claims, then renovated its structure.

Our candid confessions swept away all those old fashioned taboos, all those petty notions and nonsenses that proliferate in a conventional marriage.

We were not attempting to create or promote a permissive society. We were trying to eliminate hypocrisy.

We set out to show that a New Age of Enlightenment had dawned. An age in which bisexuals and homosexuals could find acceptance instead of living their lives in fear of ridicule and intimidation.

We were not reluctant to share with others who came into our lives the love that David and I expressed for one another.

We formed liaisons with those we worked with: singers, musicians and artists from the footlights of the entertainment profession.

We made love with people we adored and cared for.

Our acts of sexual liberation were hardly perverse. They were tender and beautiful moments. Ours were dreams of sexual freedom.

I understood David's ambivalent nature, as I am sure he recognised mine.

Inevitably, there were friends we were both attracted to, but even in these circumstances, we refused to allow jealousy to harm the other's pursuits. Nor would we try to win affection at the expense of each other.

When David found a new friend I rejoiced in his happiness and likewise, he in mine.

These were the halcyon days of our marriage, when we broke down the rigid barriers of an institution that was strangled by cobwebs.

We followed the light of truth.

Many people have since asked why we bothered to get married in the first place.

"You could have lived the way you did without that piece of paper," said one.

I imagine we could have done.

There were many reasons why we chose to marry rather than to embark on a live-in relationship and they will become apparent in the pages ahead, but there was one factor more vital than the others.

While I was in love with David and ready to share him with anyone he nominated, I still wanted to hold that privileged and treasured place as his wife.

I was prepared to bow to convention that much.

I wish now I had subscribed to convention more, because it would take its natural revenge.

And the battle we had won was not to be a victory for us personally. Our happiness faded, but for others, as the taboos and hypocrisy surrounding homosexual relationships were lifted, the light of love swept in.

1

Today, tomorrow, yesterday
Are geographical locations
In time's abhorrent calendar
Where there are no vacations.

You may stop the video and so rewind
Reel your tape to the beginning
Time has no time for these mechanics
For Youth is a mirrored senility
caught grinning.

I wonder if it's possible
To make old time a friend
Thus acquiring the wisdom
We'll need at judgements' end.

How do you tell a father that you've been expelled from college for having a lesbian affair? I couldn't say, "Dad, it's your fault because I promised I'd stay a virgin till I was 18."

I left it to my poor mother to explain why I had given boys a miss.

My father, Colonel George Milton Barnet, who collected practically every medal minted for fighting the Japanese in the Philippines during World War II, was already in despair over my schooling and this latest episode might have been too much for him to have accepted from me.

My childhood had been a strictly conventional one.

My parents were fine, proud Americans who lived in Cyprus where, after the war, my father ran the mill at a mining company at Xeros.

If he had stayed in the U.S. Army he would have been promoted to the rank of General, but my father did not subscribe to the principle of peacetime armies and he took his discharge.

Unfortunately, Cyprus was not the most peaceful haven he could have chosen to settle his family. The country was in a constant state of unrest between the British Empire and the opposing Greek and Turkish native population, and the troubles were at their peak in the late summer of 1949 when I was born.

There were only two of us children and my brother Milton John was already sixteen years old by the time I was delivered into the world.

I was christened Mary-Angela, names in keeping with the family's Catholic status. My

2

mother, Helena Marie, who was only 5 foot 2 inches tall, was from Poland's lost territory of Galizia and her family had found their way to the States.

My father, of British parentage, was tall by comparison and he was also rather handsome. I always thought he bore a resemblance to Lawrence of Arabia from the pictures I had studied.

His moustache was clipped in the classic military style and in nature he was stern and pragmatic. But if on the field of battle he could bark orders to a regiment of men, then he found it extremely difficult to force the same authority on mother.

When my mother's artistic temperament was aroused, she was more than a match for him.

To see my father being rebuked by this tiny woman was an hysterical sight. She once brandished a frying pan over him and finally cracked it down on the back of his head, according to family legend.

They would feud, not over domestic issues, but on matters affecting politics, commerce and religion. They were like a pair of intellectual eggheads at either end of the scale.

From this environment, I was bright and not afraid of anyone—teachers, other children, classmates . . . anyone! I possessed a grasshopper mind, always leaping ahead of what the teachers were trying to drill into me.

The school came under the wing of the Mining Corporation, like the church, the hospital and the social club. Things were pretty cosmopolitan with Australians, Canadians, British and Americans as well as Cypriots all working on the mining project.

3

There weren't too many girls in my glass, and for a long spell I was the only one among fourteen boys: hardly a situation to encourage anyone but the most prankish tomboy.

Our house was on the Northern coast of the island in the village of Xeros, thirty-five miles west of Kyrenia, an old red and white Colonial house with a view of the mountain peaks behind.

My parents were comfortably-off, and employed casual staff to help organise the domestic chores in the house. We were only a mile away from the headquarters of the British peace-keeping force. My father, with his military record, would often be invited as a guest to the various functions that the military staged there.

Naturally, there was always conversation about our "real" home in the States and when I was seven years old it was decided to send me there with my mother so that I could take my first Holy Communion at a Catholic school in Boise, Idaho, where some of our relatives continued to live.

In the year I stayed with my mother in America, I found I missed my schoolfriends in Cyprus and I was glad when we returned. I loved Cyprus and the sunshine and I grew up always wishing I had been born a true-blooded Cypriot. I just felt so much affection for the friendly Cypriots and their way of life.

It was sad there was so much conflict between the Turkish and Cypriot factions and through my childhood the island seemed to be in a state of civil war.

My parents, being American, could not take sides. But they could not always help being caught in the centre of the conflict. In the 1964 uprising a jet plane strafed our home

4

and as it whistled overhead, my mother scrambled protectively over me on the floor.

In the harbour a Cypriot submarine was blown out of the water and people who worked for my father were killed on the jetty.

My parents also escaped with their lives when a sniper shot at their car one night and the bullets shattered two of its windows. My mother was cut by flying glass but fortunately it left no permanent scars.

Several British regiments, before Independence, occupied the Army barracks and the sight of soldiers out on patrol was common to us as children.

The Army organised local children's parties at Christmas-time and it was the regimental mascot—a wily-eyed goat—who always stole the show. He once propelled me through the air on to a soldier's lap and later tossed me over a hedge!

When I was nine years old, my parents decided to send me to boarding school.

There were no schools for young ladies with boarding facilities and so I would have to go to England or Switzerland. My mother knew Switzerland was closer!

The day of departure came all too soon and I remember sobbing against the lining of my mother's fur coat, grief-stricken by the thought of leaving home.

My blonde hair, which I wore in ringlets, had been specially cut so that I could manage it on my own.

My mother had chosen and packed all my necessary clothes.

There was, of course, an obligatory school uniform in dove grey and white, with navy blue blazers, pleated skirts and long white socks. Pencil-line skirts were forbidden.

Like most boarding schools, there were many rules and regulations. No stiletto heels —they made bullet-like marks in the linoleum—no chewing gum, no swearing, no playing jacks on hall tables and only two to a piano box during practice!

The school, St. George's, standing high above Lake Geneva at Clarens near Montreux, was starkly foreboding to young eyes.

There were 150 girls at the school of 53 nationalities who had come from all parts of the world. The majority of them were boarders and predictably they came from wealthy homes.

I imagine that I came from a poorer background by comparison. What was more, I was also the youngest, for mother had persuaded the headmistress, Miss Georgina Codrington, to admit me a year earlier than the normal admission age.

My first year was miserable. I was constantly homesick and pined for my Mum and Dad. But in time I began to conquer my tears and slowly but surely began to enjoy my life there.

Because of the mixed nationalities, lessons were conducted in English and in French on alternate weeks. For some pupils, who originated from the Far East, or from Brazil, this meant they were having to learn two new languages immediately if they were to converse.

The youngest of us slept in dormitories with six beds to a room and again, there were certain procedures to follow, which included a ritual letter home to be written on Sunday evenings when a period of solitude was observed.

I remember Schuyler Van Johnson, who

6

was the daughter of the famous American actor Van Johnson. As kids we were all green with envy for Schuyler would receive four or five letters and cards from her father some days—and in fact most days! She was a smart, smiling, quiet girl who was great at athletics.

Normally, the school staff didn't vet our letters home, which was just as well, because I am sure they would have been shocked.

There was, however, one exceptional case when Miss O'Grady, the school dragon, endeavoured to intercept a letter written by a pint-sized Ecuadorian girl who answered to the fascinating name of Amparo Valdieveso.

Amparo objected when Miss O'Grady leaned over to take the letter from her desk and shouted at her: "How dare you read my letter."

Miss O'Grady retaliated and slapped Amparo's face but the diminutive Latin girl, whose hand in marriage was promised at the age of 13, wasn't going to be silenced. She hit the teacher back and together they sprawled over a desk, fighting one another in a scene more reminiscent of St. Trinians.

Miss O'Grady was sacked and disappeared from our lives and Amparo became the heroine of the school.

My own conflicts with the staff were rare but I was not altogether liked, especially by those teachers in whose subjects I failed to show any kind of aptitude.

I would constantly hear comments like: "You're clever Mary-Angela, so why don't you understand?"

But for me the issues always became personal ones, and if I didn't like a teacher —then I would not make any attempt to rectify the situation, relying on the warmer links I enjoyed with those teachers who were able to lead my studies in the right direction.

My father was visibly dismayed by my apparent lack of progress in maths and Latin. My results were abysmal. He could not comprehend that I failed to find any means of communication with Miss McKenna who taught both subjects in such a prim fashion that I found the lessons too complicated for me to grasp.

Only then did my father bemoan the cost of keeping me at St. George's and he would lecture me on the need to show more discipline.

I was not a rebel at school, but a "motivator".

The headmistress left me in charge of a Hallowe'en party for which I enlisted six other girls to form a Persian tableau with sedan chairs bearing a Prince and Princess, with nubile slaves in attendance. It was a scenario that won praise from the staff, but we lost one of the cast, a Pakistani pupil named Nasrine, very soon afterwards. She used to have religious visions in her sleep. One night we rescued her as she attempted to walk off the balcony "into the arms of God" and she was quickly shepherded back to Karachi, where she had a foster mother.

I took ballet lessons during all my days in Switzerland, and I excelled in the class. Madame Von Knorring said I was blessed with "Pavlova's feet" and looked on my future as a ballerina. But by thirteen, I was growing much too tall ever to train seriously as a ballerina and it was a sad realisation. Classical ballerinas were traditionally small in stature and I was already 5 foot 4 inches. I was to grow another four and half inches before reaching my full adult height. I loved ballet, and later practised in jazz and modern ballet, at the Dance Centre in London's Floral Street, but I knew that I could never make a career in it, which was the only penalty I found in life for being too tall.

The one alternative was acting, in which my teachers in Switzerland also thought I showed promise. They felt I should go to England to study. Auditions for the Royal Academy of Dramatic Art and the Central School of Drama were listed, but my father simply wouldn't hear of it. In his view, all actresses had "round heels", an expression that I wasn't familiar with and only learned what it meant years later.

Unfortunately, most parents hold that tarnished opinion of the acting profession and my father rejected out of hand the "disgusting" suggestion that I should even consider becoming an actress.

Showbusiness was always glamorous to me and like most children I was fascinated by artists and entertainers.

Returning home on leave I had met both Liberace and Renata Tebaldi aboard the Queen Mary when crossing the Atlantic. Liberace actually came to say goodnight to me in our cabin, because I wasn't old enough to have dinner at the captain's table! But I was allowed to stay up to see his last performance as the liner nosed into New York —what a treat it was.

Liberace wore one of his glittering jackets and he told the funniest stories. In my eyes he was an idol and when I thought about becoming an actress I thought about him, because he epitomised all that was good in the entertainment profession.

So the prospect of going into showbusiness didn't hold any fears for me, but I could not fight my father and I blamed him for ruining my career from that point on.

"I had the opportunity to go to England and study and you lost it for me," I said accusingly, not realising at the time that he was only trying to act in my best interests.

I stayed in Switzerland to continue my studies and the staff soothed my sorrows by making me a prefect and appointing me as the president of the social fund-raising committee.

One summer, I ran a kebab and hamburger barbecue to raise funds for charities supported by the school.

Harder studies were ahead however, as examinations loomed.

Now that my father had destroyed my ambitions to become an actress, I was bereft of any ideas for my future.

One of my aunts was a lawyer and my father tried to channel me in that direction, but the legal profession was too sombre a spectre to contemplate.

I told my father I needed to deliberate further.

I left St. George's at 16 with eight O levels and four A levels in English, French, history and history of art and I returned to join my parents in Cyprus.

I had always gone back there during summer holidays and when I was 14, I had fallen in love with a young artist named Sidney Anderson who was all of 19. My first kiss was really the biggest event of my life, passionately exchanged in the back row of a jasmine

10

scented open-air cinema during a Tony Hancock film!

My father was very disciplined about boy friends. Living in Cyprus, he liked to impose the Cypriot customs where a girl, until she was 18, had to be escorted by her mother or a chaperone.

My only brush with the opposite sex at boarding school had been when we would meet with boys from the neighbouring school at the local tuck shop or find ourselves opposing them in debating societies and sharing the platform at seminars.

But Sidney Anderson was my dream and when I left school I could think of no one else. My parents, however, had other plans for me. They thought I should go to university immediately and were happy when I gained a place at Connecticut College for Women, which meant my immediate departure for the USA.

Waiting for a place in an English university could have meant a year's delay, and my father wasn't enamoured by that prospect. Connecticut resolved the matter perfectly in his mind.

Unfortunately, I didn't take to Connecticut too well. The American college campus was totally alien to all I had experienced in Switzerland, where I assessed the level of education to be infinitely higher.

Connecticut crammed in eight lessons a day. As a college it was widely respected in the field of art and dance, but I eventually questioned this reputation in my own mind from all that I was to experience there as an undergraduate.

I'll accept I was spoilt and was accustomed to a more sophisticated style of education.

11

In Switzerland we had maids to look after us: in Connecticut we not only had to look after our own chores but those of the college too. All students were expected to staff the dining hall and I complained that I had not been sent there to train as a waitress. Nor, I said, was I telephonist when I was given a rota for operating the college switchboard.

By then I was truly established as a rebel in the eyes of the college authorities, and I could feel a certain hostility that was being directed towards me, which in turn, affected my general studies.

Despite my father's objections to me becoming an actress, I joined the College drama society and throughout my stay at Connecticut this was the only memory for which I have any fondness.

One of the productions I took part in was an adaptation of Thomas Middleton's "The Changeling" and while Connecticut provided the female members of the cast, Yale nominated the male leads.

Playing opposite me was Joey, an Italian boy with dark curly hair, and witty sense of humour.

Soon we were dating and all the members of the company regarded me as Joey's girl.

I'm afraid that Joey must have found it a little frustrating.

I'd promised my father that I wouldn't get "into any kind of trouble" and in making that rash pledge I realised the implications, but I wasn't going to cheat.

I decided to hang on to my virginity until I was 18, and after that what could my father really do about it? I should be able to make my own decisions at that age.

Joey lost patience with me and I really

couldn't blame him. Petting wasn't going far enough, not when kids all over the campus were already having affairs. There were plenty of other girls he could make it with.

Until that point, I have been aware of my physical and social needs and behaved accordingly within certain moral boundaries, but I had yet to fall in love to know that great surge of energy from deep in your soul at the mere sight of a treasured face. To describe love is to attempt the impossible.

The person I fell in love with was a girl.

I first saw Lorraine in the dining hall. A tall, thin blonde in butch, denim clothes. Not beautiful, but positively eccentric-looking.

For some reason I could not explain, I was excited by her.

This was the first time I'd ever got emotional about a girl and I tried to dismiss it from my thoughts. But the more I looked at Lorraine the more I became fascinated by her.

She was sitting opposite me at lunch in the dining hall the next day. It was too much of a coincidence and my heart pounded, but again I couldn't fathom the reason for it.

But now I was talking to her, quickly exchanging stereotype questions. . . . "How long have you been here?" "Where do you come from?" and then chatting more comfortably with one another as we found interest growing.

Lorraine liked my European background and as an artist about to take her degree she was impressed to think that I had been to Florence in travels with my family.

When we gazed into one another's eyes, a strange feeling came over me. I felt an irresistible urge to kiss her.

13

I couldn't begin to understand why and I had to stop my thoughts from running away. I could find no logical explanation.

I had never been excited by a girl before. I was not aware of "harbouring lesbian tendencies"—a term that had been like a battle-cry from the protective Miss Codrington at St. George's in Switzerland who was known to raise this theme at her luncheon table to certain staff and members of the school.

I don't think any of us ever really learned the truth behind her warnings, but I know we were all very suspicious about a staff supervisor, a big, big momma who would "entertain" her favourite pupils in her room.

I knew I could not quell my feelings when I thought of Lorraine.

She was in another part of the college but I got to see her at every opportunity I could.

When I went to bed I dreamed only of her and I became totally obsessive about her.

Finally, I became decisive.

I just knew that Lorraine wouldn't turn me away, if I told her how I felt. I was sure our feelings were mutual.

I began scheming as to how I could make it happen, but fate took a hand.

I bumped into Lorraine one morning after rehearsals with the Drama Society.

We nodded at one another and we both knew what we were going to do. Lorraine had her own room and she took me to it.

The door closed behind us.

We made love—sweeping all our frustrations aside. All the constrictions of my upbringing were swept away.

I had discovered the meaning of love. And of sex. I enjoyed orgasm because I knew there was no danger of becoming pregnant.

14

This wasn't Lorraine's first experience, although I hardly cared at the time.

I had fallen in love with Lorraine and at sixteen years of age I was blind to the consequences.

Suddenly, I was the centre of a scandal that swept the campus. I couldn't hide my feelings for Lorraine and I didn't care who knew.

What were they upset about?

The teachers were subdued but I soon got to hear that the college senate was outraged by my behaviour. Just who did this European upstart think she was? How many other undergraduates' affairs would become public and probably scandalous if brought out into the open as they would do if she continued to flout convention and authority? She had to be stopped.

I wasn't interested in listening to the grapevine feedback.

My affair with Lorraine was immune to the stares and the knowing smiles of other students. I was oblivious to what they were all thinking. Lorraine adopted the same attitude.

We had been lovers for three months when we reached the point of no return. Maybe I got too claustrophobic but one afternoon Lorraine just freaked out.

One minute we were talking to each other and the next minute she'd gone from the room. She gave no explanation at all.

I went searching for her and in my travels collided with the House Monitor whom we called Muffin.

"So there you are," she said, as if she had been looking for me. "We're worried about you. It's Lorraine, we've admitted her to the infirmary."

"Are you crazy?" I retorted "I was with her a couple of hours ago and there was nothing wrong with her."

She grimaced.

"Lorraine came to us because she is very depressed and upset about you . . ."

"Okay," I said, "I'll come over and pick her up."

I marched across to the red-brick infirmary on the far side of the campus and as I entered, I was suddenly aware that I had walked into a trap. Two nursing assistants and a woman psychiatrist were waiting for me.

They grabbed hold of me. One of them stuck a hypodermic needle into my arm. As I began to lose consciousness, I screamed but all I saw before I passed out were the faces of my assailants.

It must have been two days before I woke. My eyes suddenly focused on a white ceiling and I found that I had been strapped to a bed in an upper room of the infirmary.

A nurse moved forward into view and she asked: "How are you feeling?"

I said: "Where am I? What happened? Where is Lorraine?"

The nurse started talking to me and when she touched my arm and straightened the pillow I sensed that she cared.

"Look," I said, "I'm aching all over. Why not unstrap me and let me sit up? What can I do? I can't run away from here."

She nodded and helped me up in the bed. I smiled affectionately towards her and then said: "Couldn't I just put on my trousers? I feel stupid the way I am now."

She picked my trousers up from a chair and watched me climb into them, her eyes not

16

missing a single movement. I threw on the rest of my clothes and then sat talking to her.

I got up and drifted over to the window, to check exactly where I was being held, and saw the lawn running not far below. I turned to the nurse and began to protest. "You know you are holding me here against my will? What do you think will happen to you all when I tell my parents how you injected me with a hypodermic needle?" She flushed and said: "It was for your own good."

I asked: "What happened to Lorraine? Are you keeping her here as well?"

It was clear to me, from the conversation, that we were being intimidated deliberately because our relationship opposed the conventional standards set by the College senate.

Suddenly I had the urge to escape. I went to the window and threw it open. Before the nurse could stop me, I leaped through and jumped to the ground some ten or twelve feet below.

My legs crumpled as I hit the lawn but fortunately the turf was soft and I got up and fled like a prisoner escaping jail.

I ran to Lorraine's room and gasping for breath, I collapsed panting.

"What happened to you? Where have you been?"

"I'm sorry Angie," she replied, "I've been trying to see you but they wouldn't let me come in."

"Lorraine," I cried, "don't you see? We are being victimised for loving each other. Ours is a kind of relationship that they can't accept."

I had barely finished speaking when a posse of security police arrived with Muffin.

"Well now," she exclaimed, "what's happening here?"

17

I took one step forward, now able to cope with the situation because I wasn't going to take any more foolishness from them.

"Don't touch me," I remonstrated. "You are not going to drug me again. You're going to have to get one of these men to shoot me first and that won't look very good for Connecticut College for Women."

Muffin shrank back in fear of my attack. She knew I would cause a scandal otherwise.

"All right," she said, "calm down. You can go back to your own room, but I still think you should take a tranquiliser. You're too upset to know what you are doing."

I returned to my room and fell into an uneasy sleep, still wondering what would happen next. The answer was swift in coming. I was called into the principal's office the next morning and shown a copy of a letter that had been sent to my parents, telling them of my expulsion from college for forming "an unhealthy relationship with other students".

Arrangements were speedily made for me to leave college and a few days later I flew home to Cyprus.

While I felt no shame or stigma, a certain apprehension crept upon me as the plane landed in Nicosia and my parents thrust forward to greet me. I think I was slightly nervous at the prospect of having to explain to them what the term "an unhealthy relationship" might be interpreted as meaning.

Luckily they didn't ask any probing questions and discretion was exercised.

I could read my father's consternation, however, and I guess mother told him the

18

truth of the affair, for it was felt judicious to send me on to London with mother as chaperone.

My "penance" in London was to enrol at an Oxford Street secretarial college for a short-hand and typewriting course.

I had to find some way to placate my father who read the word "expulsion" as "ruination".

My mother and I checked into the White House, a service suite hotel at the gates of Regents Park.

Suddenly some letters turned up from Cyprus which had been forwarded to us.

My mother opened mine by mistake and one glance at her flustered face was enough to tell me who they were from.

Lorraine was a pretty descriptive writer. To her, writing a letter was like painting a picture, or making love.

I guess my mother knew everything, but she didn't challenge me. She just set about trying to cure me from my bad habits in her own old-fashioned way.

When we went home to Cyprus for the summer vacation she invited every eligible boy in the district to woo me!

Lorraine didn't exactly disappear from my life, but when I next saw her it was something of a surprise.

Six years had gone by and I was still married to David. We were on a concert tour of the States.

I thought it would be nice to see Lorraine again and I traced her when we were in New York.

She was living in Newhaven and it was wonderful to see her. She had not changed at all. Her artistic talent was still the dominant force in her life and she worked from one exhibition to another.

Sadly, her parents and Connecticut College had sentenced her to four years in mental institutions after I had left.

I cried as she told me of the sufferings she had experienced, but in my heart I thanked her for having made me realise that I had been right in taking a stand on all relationships between free spirits.

Some people are always free. Their relationships must be the movement and communication of free spirits.

I knew that as soon as a relationship became categorised as being outside the law or society, we were constricting our own moral values and becoming inconsistent with the will of God.

That day she told me that our affair in Connecticut had changed her life.

"Angie," she whispered as we made love once more, "I am really happy now."

"I know you are, my first love," I said.

I guess David would have understood.

2

*Sometimes as night closes day
and welcomes darkness, it is too early
to sink into dreams' repose
and you cannot quieten the thoughts
occurring to you.*

Girls weren't going to dictate my life. There was a whole world ready and waiting for me and whatever I had to offer. I had no desire to put limitations on my thoughts, words or ambitions. I had started to write poetry for Lorraine, able to fill the absent spaces by transcribing my thoughts and presenting them to her. She was my first audience.

Would I find another audience any better than she to receive my inspiration, devotion and physical loyalty?

These were the questions that needed answering but there was time. So much time.

It never lay easily on my hands. My mother and father knew that in my case I had to be fully occupied all of the time, so my mother kept me company as I finished my Oxford Street secretarial course. She also helped me process my application to Kingston Polytechnic to read for a degree in economics or a higher national diploma in business studies —whichever came first, I thought!

It was there that I met Bill. He was a big, rugged Yorkshireman. He was 25 years old and he was taking his masters degree in economics.

English humour was so different from American. It was basic but honest.

Bill did not know of my pledge with myself to remain a virgin until I was 18, so assuaging my filial and Catholic guilt. He finally caught up with the gossip.

"So you're the good Catholic girl waiting for the witching hour?" he teased, "and we've got two days to go . . ."

It maybe hard to accept, because of past events in Connecticut, but I blushed!

My embarrassment mounted by the hour.

The day of my birthday arrived. Jill, my

room mate, and I went to the Students' Union pub for lunch. Bill was there and shyly offered me two small boxes. They contained pairs of diamante earrings, just the kind I liked, long and dangly. He said he would pick me up from the hostel to go to Hampton Wick, a nearby village, for a drink.

Everyone was there.

Over hearty pints of strong English bitter their "Happy Birthday" merriment soon gave way to music hall quips. "It's gonna be tonight . . ." they laughed.

I didn't know where to hide my face, as friends began to slap Bill on the back. They were sending him off to perform.

Bill's car, an Austin Healey, stood out on the forecourt and we were jostled towards it.

We were like a couple who were going on honeymoon and I suddenly realised that Bill was taking things much more seriously than I could have contemplated.

He grabbed hold of me and gave me a pinch.

"So you think it is going to be tonight?" he said, and laughed.

Bill started the engine and accelerated away in a roar of exhaust as I tried to gather my thoughts.

"I thought that as we're going to marry, you had better come up to Yorkshire and meet my parents," said Bill.

Marry? Did Bill say marry? That hadn't been my idea at all. How had I given him that impression?

"Does going to bed with you mean we have to marry?" I asked nervously.

"Well, that's what you must have in mind," shrugged Bill.

I didn't answer, but I could not disguise a sigh.

Bill came from a farming family and on the journey he told me that his grandmother ran four corner stores in villages scattered all over the county.

I could tell he was very proud of his background.

I had never been to Yorkshire before, but even in the darkness I could feel the freshness of the countryside.

His parents stayed up to meet me. They were warm and gentle people, as I knew farming people to be, and so was his grey-haired grandmother who toasted us some bread on a long toasting fork over the charcoal grate.

One of the bedrooms was made ready for me and I fell asleep in the early hours. My eighteenth birthday had gone and I was still a virgin!

I woke at dawn to the crowing of cockerels and I gazed out of the lattice window overlooking the hills. I saw hay ricks and grazing cattle.

The appetising smell of fried eggs and bacon wafted from the kitchen and I heard voices below. I got dressed and made my way down the narrow staircase.

Bill was in the kitchen watching his mother cook and after breakfast he was ready to take me on a tour of the farm. It was dotted with tractors, threshers and other equipment.

Late afternoon we drove back to London and to Bill's flat in Raynes Park. It was a cosy little apartment.

Bill wasn't anxious to waste any more time, and neither was I, but I held growing reservations.

I had to be honest to myself. I didn't share

with Bill any kind of emotional or spiritual understanding.

With Lorraine it was a spiritually satisfying experience. But I couldn't turn back. I wouldn't turn back.

Bill was lying on the sofa watching television, waiting for me. I don't know how girls can tell things like this. I sidled over to the sofa, my best Lauren Bacall profile thrust forward, and as I slid under his arm, I realised I'd always be an actress in B-movies, but I could see the Humphrey Bogart in his chin.

The passing of time was punctuated by mugs of tea, snacks of egg and chips, beans on toast and grilled mushroom sandwiches, as two days turned into one long, highly-educational moment of truth.

Added to which I had an opportunity to observe somebody who was totally different from myself. Bill was a strange, interesting character for me. He was terribly bright and had no reason to devote any time to his studies. He handled them all with such ease, examinations and assignments alike. He was specialising in marketing and I could listen to him talk and argue with his friends for hours, assimilating campaigns and promotions and marketing techniques. It all fascinated me. I adored people with ready, open minds who could vocalise their innermost thoughts and their outermost ambitions. There was so much talking going on, fortunately I had the good sense to do all the listening. I wanted a crash course on life and Bill gave it to me.

But telling Bill that I wasn't going to marry him took some doing. Gradually he got the message. Whenever friends enquired as friends do, I'd tell them that I wanted to enjoy some time of freedom before getting married. It was slightly hurtful, but I didn't mean it to be: Bill had rather brought it upon himself by assuming we would marry and not consulting me first.

I still bear fond memories of him and let's be honest—how fabulous to be introduced to the joys of carnal knowledge by a big strapping intelligent hunk of Yorkshireman.

In fact, when in later years I returned to England to live and the train rumbled through Raynes Park, I would break into fits of laughter to think I had conceded my finest moment somewhere under those grey rooftops of suburbia!

In my first year at the Polytechnic, after sharing a room with Jill in the women's student hostel, she and I moved to a bed sitter in Surbiton.

Even Charles Dickens might have been hard put to describe the degradation and poverty suffered by students studying in the depths of English suburbia in 1968!

Our bed sitter was a real trip. The one living room was graced by a threadbare carpet, broken armchairs and a couple of single beds with sunken, uncomfortable mattresses. Wallpaper peeled from the walls and dampness rose in the corners. The bathroom and kitchen were somehow curiously combined. The bathtub itself had a retractable lid that was meant to serve as a working surface for kitchen use! An eye level water-heater took pride of place and next to it was sited the gas cooker. All of this for seven pounds a week!

But accommodation was that scarce that we were grateful to find it and Jill and I were resigned to making the best of it. This was our first going-it-alone solo pad, footloose and fancy free!

My father gave me an allowance—indeed, he began to send me congratulatory notes when I got through a term's examination hurdles. I had restored his pride in me and my expulsion from Connecticut was now a chapter in the past.

My thirst for knowledge was sharpening. It's nothing to do with what you're learning, it is the actual atmosphere and the environment.

In England it is especially clever because the atmosphere is precisely tempered. As soon as you walk on to a university campus it's as though your senses are instantly stimulated.

In my teens I was very opinionated but as I absorbed more college life, things seemed to fall into perspective a little more. You begin to formulate what's right and what's wrong and in so doing you forge your own character.

I generated a lot of energy through this period. My attendance at lectures became secondary to a student union rally if one was called. I was fascinated by other people and their radical views. Like all students I loved the air of rebellion and anarchy and I would spend hours in the library searching for answers and ammunition.

They were funny, zany days and I remember posing for a modelling composite for a friend of mine called Steve—wonderful action shots of me running through Hyde Park in a white jump suit! It was outrageous! Too outrageous, I guess, for the established fashion houses, because I sure never got a booking!

I began to let my studies lapse and I was gallivanting around too much. Then came the real shock and one that I had not anticipated—the Polytechnic refused to allow me to take my finals because I had not attended the mandatory number of lectures.

At that point I freaked out because I didn't dare tell my father, who thought I had reformed into being a true, dedicated scholar.

Rather than face his wrath, I resolved to remain in England. I could have joined Bentall's, one of England's largest departmental stores, in their marketing division, but I didn't have a working permit.

It posed a real problem, but a boy in college whose uncle managed a tourist night club in London found a temporary loophole for me. I could work at the club, booking holiday travel for club members, and drawing expenses instead of wages. I wasn't au fait with the law but I was assured it was all legitimate. So I took the job.

If I had considered life in college was wild and riotous, then my experiences at the Nomad Travel Club in Sussex Gardens were almost beyond description. Staff rooms were above the club and I shared one with a carrot-haired Australian girl called Dinx. In the next room were a pair of girl bartenders, while three Mexicans who formed the band were spread out in noisy rooms above us.

Booking holiday travel was a joke, although when guests staggered into the club in varying states of intoxication from the cellar disco, it was much easier to convince them that they needed a holiday "away from it all".

I would promptly sell them immediate all-in weekends to Ibiza or to Majorca for forty-nine pounds. Once they paid the cash I would give them a receipt and they would then be passed onto a booking office to make the final arrangements.

Most nights there would be an eruption of some kind in the club. If it wasn't a customer complaining about his bar bill, then it would be a drunk who would be grappling with the bouncers before hitting the pavement.

One of the waitresses became pregnant by the Mexican bass player whose mother arrived to escort them back to Mexico to get married. Then the drummer jumped out of a second floor window but instead of committing suicide as he intended, he bounced off a passing car and suffered concussion. . .

My friend's uncle was a Lebanese wrestler and I liked working for him. The owner, a South African, spent most of his time trying to make his wife, a dreadful singer, into a star.

Many agents and better-known entertainers would be dragged along to hear her sing. They never returned. Terribly bad for business!

Whenever I had a night off I would go to the theatre.

I still wanted to be an actress, but I knew it was going to be difficult to break through. Without a working permit, my prospects of joining the actors' union, Equity, were practically zero.

In any event, the trail through the remote regions of repertory wasn't too tempting.

There seemed to be no short cuts, but that's when "Doctor" Calvin Mark Lee came into my life. Calvin, who was running the European offices for Mercury Records, was a figure of some notoriety.

Indeed, he was regarded in the music world like an Oriental prince, for his looks alone gave him that kind of presence. Of Chinese origin, he wore a silver love jewel on the forehead of his arresting face which was framed by long, dark hair.

Calvin would come and see me in the club and we would talk for hours.

"I want to be an actress," I told him, "but it seems the prospects are hopeless."

"Come out with me," he said, "we'll have a laugh, I know a lot of people who might be able to help you. You've got to meet the *right people*."

Calvin was a character and fun to be with. He took me out to London's best places to meet agents, directors and producers. It seemed like star-spotting to me!

I really liked Calvin and he made no demands on me. It was a nice, easy-going relationship.

He was excited about a new singer his record company were about to put under contract.

"What is his name?" I asked.

"David Bowie," replied Calvin, "and he is marvellous. I will take you to see him."

Seeing David for the first time on the stage of London's Roundhouse, my sympathies spilled over for Calvin. Who could not lose their heart to someone with so much charisma?

A lean, blond, enigmatic figure in a pastel-striped sweater and mustard-coloured sailor's flares and a voice so compelling that no-one could turn a head, David captivated every single member of the audience.

Every move, every gyration quickened the pulse. His steel blue eyes burned with mystery that defied the searching spotlights and his whole performance exuded an eroticism that hung over the auditorium thicker than the layers of cigarette smoke.

David was singing with a group named

Feathers and a girl singer also featured in the act—Hermione, a lissom, auburn-haired creature who had once been a ballet dancer and, it later transpired, David's first love who was the subject of one of his tracks, "Letter to Hermione".

The exhilaration of that night left me reeling. It was my first rock 'n' roll concert. On the same bill were The Who and the dry-witted Scaffold, but they were all very different from David Bowie, whose aesthetic qualities made him stand out alone.

Backstage after the show, Calvin pushed and prodded me through a cordon of well-wishers surrounding David. Our hands barely clasped in the hustle and bustle of a dressing room that resembled a sardine tin.

It would not be long before we met again.

Calvin arranged dinner in Chinatown.

We were an intimate threesome. The conversation seemed to flow steadily and clearly. David and Calvin were discussing the Mercury recording contract which would allow David to release first a single, "Space Oddity", to be produced by Gus Dudgeon and then an album which would be produced by his friend Tony Visconti.

Lou Reisner was Calvin's direct superior in Mercury Records and I had gone out with him while I was at Kingston Polytechnic. We had met in an elevator at Leonard's the hairdressers. A very small elevator, I might add. He had to stoop to get in and, towering over me, he began talking to me and I could not escape until I promised to have lunch with him the following day. Through my friendship with Lou Reisner I gradually became acquainted with marvellous people in the music business, among them a Welsh band called The Eyes of

Gloom who were signed to Mercury, and Buzzy Linhart, an American folk artist who recorded several albums in London.

We would go down to the studio to visit as albums ground to completion. Buddy Miles came to town and recorded an L.P. with Lou and his company.

Telly Savalas also recorded an album and Lou took me to lunch with him and his wife. They were charming people. Telly had a wonderful musical talent, and a great acting ability which he came to display in films and television. Who was to know he would become Kojak?

At this period I also met Enrico Macias who came into London for several television shows. I never knew Enrico's ethnic extraction but one or the other of his parents was from Algeria and he had a haunting, melodic grasp of rhythm. I loved his songs.

Lou was very proud in being the London-based executive for Enrico's recording company.

Everything was exciting and different and new. I soaked it up like a sponge. I had applied my marketing theories and techniques to the conversations I listened to.

Now talking with Calvin and David at dinner I felt as if events had been ordered so that somehow we might have arrived at this moment.

We decided to go from supper on to a club. I had been to the Speakeasy before with Calvin. But it all seemed special that night. The people seemed livelier, the dancers were better, the audience more animated and beautifully dressed. An atmosphere of excitement hung in the club.

We took our seats and as the lights dimmed

I whispered to David that we were at some sort of private party or function.

"I know," he whispered back, "I can't think why they let us in."

But I knew why.

David was special. Very special. He would always be let in wherever he wanted to go.

The lights dimmed and the band, who were the talk of London started to play. A band called King Crimson. They were devastating, so loud, such melodies, true musical arrangements yet with a thudding rock 'n' roll underbeat. They played a whole set and at the end we were exhausted with excitement.

Calvin and David and I ordered drinks. People went on the floor to dance. We just sat talking, the three of us, marvelling at the wonderful performance we had just seen.

Various people came by the table to greet David, but all eyes were on the stage as the band came back to play the second set. Suddenly we heard the introduction and King Crimson announced Donovan. Out he walked and the place trembled. The music started and as Donovan began his performance the club went nuts.

"Do you jive?" David asked me.

"Jive?" I said "Certainly."

So we got up and started to dance. God it was great. It's fabulous when two people who have been trained as dancers, no matter under what circumstances, whether it be studio or night club, get a chance to dance together for the first time.

We were very good that night. We must have looked great, too. I was wearing my purple velvet three-piece trouser suit and wild fuchsia silk shirt with purple silk tie.

David was stunning in T-shirt and trousers,

just like a jazz dancer practising in a studio.

Funnily enough, I had not talked to Calvin about David. I knew that he was professionally devoted to David's work and loved him as a friend.

Calvin had a rogues' gallery of photographs of all his friends and it became a guessing game for me to spot those with whom he'd had affairs.

For my part, I fancied Calvin like anything.

I used to lie on Calvin's bed and look at the photographs of David. They were gorgeous pictures. He was so handsome . . . later David was quoted as saying "When we met we were both laying the same bloke."

It might have been true, but I never thought about it like that. Calvin was somehow a great friend and kindred spirit. He fed and revitalised the social life of a lot of aspiring young talent in London at the time. David and I were among hundreds of his friends.

One didn't really see Calvin often. He was too busy. He had a very tight working schedule and he tried to spread his time among all of his friends. He was always a breath of fresh air and full of new ideas.

He had a great collection of Vassarely art prints, the acquisition of a new one was a time for visiting his studio in Lower Sloane Street and showing admiration.

That night, after the Speakeasy, I felt totally different.

I just knew that David would figure importantly and irretrievably in my life: his whole nature and being was gentle and sensitive, but in his beautifully structured face I detected so much depth and definition to his character that it cried out to be explored.

34

David promised to phone the next day and I was on tenterhooks awaiting his call. Butterflies buzzed my system and by the end of the morning I was a nervous wreck.

When eventually David got through I was almost too breathless to give an immediate coherent answer to his suggestion of dining again that night, but without Calvin.

I was not going to defy the inevitable. Nor was David. We became lovers quite naturally that evening. It seemed predestined.

Making love with David was the fulfilling experience I secretly felt I could achieve with a person—a person in whom I could find genuine love. And a man—so that anything would be possible in the terms of fulfilling a human relationship in its fullest complexity.

In the early hours, when our passions retreated, we talked of the past intimacies of our lives.

I told David the cause of my expulsion from university, but he wasn't shocked nor remotely surprised to think that I should have had an affair with a girl. He understood the meaning of it.

"You only did what you felt," he said, "that's how love is. You can't control those kind of feelings."

From his sympathetic attitude, I sensed that he must have had similar experiences but I didn't press him to tell me.

I felt singularly relieved that he could accept my liaison with Lorraine in the way he did—as though it had been a perfectly natural thing to do.

In the past I had brazenly told other boy friends about it. Sometimes I did it to wind them up. Male instincts would often be aroused, the perpetual male fantasy would

35

rear. Nothing would give a boy more pleasure than to conjure a vision of sharing a bed with two girls at play.

I am sure that David was as vulnerable to these kind of fantasies as other men, but his physical desires were finely balanced with the meaning and depth of a relationship, as I was to learn in the coming years.

At that precise moment, lying in bed for the first time together, I was ready to listen with fascination to his early life, his humble beginnings and his love for music.

He talked with enthusiasm of the experimental arts laboratory he was running in Beckenham.

He also told me about a lady named Mary Finnigan, a journalist, who was helping to run the lab with him. My heart sank. I could not bear the thought of David working so closely with somebody else.

"We work together, but we don't belong to one another," said David, trying to cushion the blow a little, "people don't belong to each other. She has her life and I have mine."

Great waves of sadness suddenly engulfed me and when David started to get dressed, ready to leave, I became quite desperate.

I didn't want him to go, the thought was unbearable and I clung to him.

"Stay here with me, David," I pleaded, "don't leave now. . . ."

David had taken my love. And my soul. How could he leave now after the night of fulfilment we had shared?

His face paled, his hands brushed my hair soothingly.

"I've got so much to do. I just can't stay here," he said. "I promise I will phone you. . . ."

He buttoned his shirt and slipped on his jacket. And suddenly he was gone.

I really thought I had lost him and I became so hysterical that I unburdened my plight to my girl friend Dinx who gave me a Valium to calm me down.

David called me at lunch time. "Are you all right?" he asked.

"Yes," I feigned, "I'm fine now. I'm sorry I caused such a fuss."

"Don't worry," he said, "I'll be over later to see you."

David arrived at last and we went out to dinner. But I didn't have dinner on my mind!

We made love. It was as tender and poignant as before. As a lover, David was totally unselfish. My satisfaction mattered as much to him as his own.

Dawn's first light arrived and David rose from the bed. He had to go.

"Where are you going?" I cried, panic-stricken. "You can't leave me again."

David sighed as he gathered his strewn clothes from the carpet.

"Angie, you don't understand," he said, "I've got to work. We've got a show on Sunday. Mary can't manage by herself. Everyone in the Arts Lab is relying on me."

I regained my senses and assured him I would be all right, but as I heard his departing steps on the stairs a sudden piece of mischief came to mind, inspired by Dinx's Valium of the day before.

I rushed to the top of the stairs, looking as if I had just swallowed a handful of pills, my sense of the dramatic never leaving me.

I then plummeted to the bottom of the stairs, never questioning the thought that David would be stopped in his tracks. Banisters hurtled past my head and I arrived at the bottom a dishevelled and crumpled heap. A pitiful sight—but not, apparently, to David.

As I groaned and looked up at him pathetically, he walked over me and said, "I will call you tomorrow. Goodbye, love . . ."

I looked after him and thought to myself: "You're so cool."

3

I feel you've got a trick
that is a Chinese puzzle game
as we tire, grow old and sick
gradually we learn its name

Questions asked are what you want
your answers given so diverse
that with philosophy you taunt
man's quest for spiritual rebirth

A whole week went by and David didn't call. When he did, it was in a whispered, almost unrecognisable voice to tell me he was dying from 'flu and could I get over to Beckenham right away?

I took a mini cab. I discovered, with some measure of surprise, that he was living in a house rented by Mary Finnigan in Foxgrove Road. He didn't have his own home. It was a thirties-style house and very comfortable.

Mary was away on a journalistic assignment and David was really in a bad way. It was a virus of some kind as he was feverish and breaking out into hot and cold shivers.

He refused all suggestion of calling in a doctor, so I went out and bought aspirin and medicines and dosed him up with them.

I also made him lemon juice and fed him soup and fruit.

By the time Mary returned a few days later he was back on his feet and he explained my presence as a friend in a Florence Nightingale cloak who had come to his rescue!

Mary, an attractive young divorcee with two children, was much smarter than that. She guessed there was more to our relationship.

She was polite but cool and I could not blame her, particularly when David suggested I should move in as I had nowhere else to live.

It was, to say the least, a delicate and complicated period.

Mary acted as the Art Lab's administrator, leaving David in the role he was best suited as artistic director.

Around them, they had built a nucleus of helpers and contributors, who recognised the Lab's objective to give an airing to new talent.

Every Sunday night various musicians and entertainers would be booked to perform on a makeshift stage—like a theatre workshop—at the nearby Three Tuns public house.

My own involvement in David's life and career was gradual, as indeed was my move from Sussex Gardens to Beckenham where I transferred my possessions, suitcase by suitcase.

David and I had our own room—once I had tidied it. Until that time it was practically impossible to get three or four feet through the door.

It was crammed with musical instruments and equipment and boxes and boxes of tapes.

Mary accepted the relationship between us with dignity and there was no hostility on her part. She resigned herself to the fact we were lovers.

We tried to stay out of the way as much as possible. We spent odd days at Tony Visconti's home, but we were pressuring ourselves to find a place of our own.

David's father, a Public Relations Director for Dr. Barnardo's Homes, became very ill with double pneumonia at this period but we did not know the extent of the crisis. We were in Italy where David was participating in a song contest.

When news came through that his father was not expected to live, David immediately returned but he was too late. His father had passed away four hours earlier.

David was deeply distressed. In some ways he blamed his mother and asked her: "Why didn't you get him into hospital?" She was too numb to give an explanation or any reason.

She was a sad, lonely figure, but not for long. When, after the funeral we were to move in with her, so that she would not be alone, she was unappreciative. It was clear she resented my presence, although I tried to be as friendly and respectful to her as possible.

Trying to help in the kitchen, which she regarded as her exclusive domain, there would be unpleasant scenes into which David would be inevitably drawn.

We just had to find a place of our own and the opportunity came when we heard of some flats in Haddon Hall, a decaying red-bricked Victorian house.

I charmed old man Hoy the landlord into accepting us as tenants of the largest vacant flat, which comprised of the hall, minstrel gallery, three large rooms, kitchen and bathroom, verandah and garden.

But before even thinking about improvements we scrubbed the tongue-and-grooved floors, once paraded upon by an octogenarian's eighteen cats, with buckets of antiseptic.

If I felt that relations with David's mother would improve, then I was wildly off the mark. She didn't like her son living in sin—it wasn't respectable.

Once the telephone was installed, our troubles mounted. David's mother was constantly calling.

The situation became intolerable and I could no longer cope with the strain. I got on a plane to Cyprus, telling David that though we were "living in sin" (these were his mother's words) I felt very deeply committed to our reationship and I did not like the constant telephonic abuse.

I spent Christmas with my parents in Xeros. I heard nothing from England. There was a postal strike and all mail deliveries were cancelled.

It must have been ten days before the postal service was resumed and all our Christmas mail arrived in the first batch.

There was a card from David and my heart missed a beat when I saw the note he had scribbled on the back. It read, "Please come back. We will marry, I promise, this year."

I showed the card to my parents. They rejoiced in my happiness, because they realised how much I was in love.

My father put his arm on my shoulder and said: "Are you sure you are going to be happy if you marry this boy?"

I just nodded.

"David is so wonderful. You'll love him when you meet him," I said.

That evening an overseas operator came on with a telephone call from England. It was David. He was worried, because I had made no response to his card.

I explained to him that I had only received it that morning. I said: "I am catching the next plane to London to be with you."

David said: "Please listen." Into the telephone he played the acetate of a new song he had composed for me. It was called "The Prettiest Star", a song that was to become a minor hit for him.

The lyrics* were very beautiful and started: "You'll be my rest and peace child" and continued, "One day, though it might be well someday, you and I will rise up all the way . . . all because of what you are—the prettiest star."

*Lyrics Copyright 1970 Design Music Ltd.

As I heard David's voice sing those tender, loving words, I just cried.

I was truly in love and I knew, in that moment, that David was in love with me.

In England, just twenty four hours later, I rushed into David's arms at London Airport. We were now committed to one another.

I think David had lectured his mother a little. He had made it clear to her that he wished to conduct his own life and that she would have to accept that I would be part of it.

David had already begun to renovate the flat at Haddon Hall.

Our bedroom had been decorated in a pastel blue and there were new furnishings, including a wardrobe and dressing table. He had also bought one or two fine pieces of art nouveau, which formed the beginning of quite a collection.

There seemed no obstacles now to our marriage but David felt compelled to go over the ground once more, like a final briefing.

David, I am sure, didn't want to deceive me about his life-style. He wanted to put it right on the line from the start so that I would not hold any illusions about our future together.

"Don't expect anything conventional Angie," said David, "because it can't be that way. I'm not made like that. I do things that other people might not subscribe to and I think it's only fair that you should know that before we set out."

David didn't choose to enlarge on that. I didn't press him, but the drift was pretty clear. I was willing to accept this man in any kind of circumstances.

I trusted him. I believed in him. He was

being as honest with me as he could be, without being blatant.

"If you can put up with the way I live, then there will be no problem," he shrugged. "We will always be together, come what may."

I would be *his*, and he would be *mine*, and I knew it was a pact that would have more meaning to him than the recitation of the marriage vows.

In the meantime, we had more pressing things to consider.

I had not worked since leaving the Nomad Travel Club, except for assisting David with the Arts Lab. We would run four-hour afternoon classes in which he would teach mime and I would lecture on improvisation and street theatre, but eventually the whole thing got too complicated for us. The attitude of the students also became very radical and a union element crept in. The Lab took the name GROWTH but one got a headache just looking at the stationery and it was time to call it a day. We withdrew from the organisation and so did Mary Finnigan, who by now had become a very good friend to me.

David's image as a singer was taking shape but managerial troubles froze his royalties and his "Space Oddity" single and album became known in the trade as "sleepers", because it wasn't until six months after their release that they finally broke into the charts.

When our wedding was arranged at Beckenham register office on March 20, 1970, my parents sent a wedding gift of a thousand dollars, most of which we put into Haddon Hall by way of carpets, curtains and other furnishings.

The day before our wedding we went to

Kensington antique market and I bought my bridal gown there—a long, silk summer dress in purple and pink.

David bought a pair of tight black satin trousers, which he was later to wear as part of his stage costume. He also put on for the ceremony a cream satin shirt with flared sleeves, and overprinted with a Prussian blue and tan floral pattern. There was no hiding the fact that we were the secondhand bride and groom; secondhand kids, utilising what had gone before—before it became a fashionable trait.

The countdown was getting closer. Most grooms arrange a stag night before their wedding day, while some brides find themselves embroiled in a hen party.

Not for us.

I suppose what we got into was something unique, and it happened on our way home from Kensington market, with our wedding robes stowed in David's Fiat car. We dropped by on a girl called Clare, one of our closest friends.

She lived in Bloomsbury and we thought it would be a nice gesture to invite her to our wedding.

Clare was a young and talented artist who had made a hit with a marvellous collection of drawings of children's faces—and her own amazing looks qualified her for a dual profession as a model.

Dark brown hair tumbled about her incredible heart-shaped face and she had a petite but perfectly contoured body.

Clare was genuinely pleased to see us and she invited us to stay for dinner. It was a magical evening and when Clare indicated we could stay the night because things had got so late, we just agreed.

Tumbling into bed seemed the right thing to do. Why break up what had been a perfect dinner party?

David had promised our marriage wasn't going to be conventional and I guess he was right with this little demonstration.

It could also have been regarded as an omen for the future, and on hindsight it was, but those kind of thoughts didn't cross my mind at the time.

I had never been to bed with a man and a woman together before. It promised to be something very special. And it was.

I wouldn't have missed the experience for the world.

What happened was so natural. When three people make love then one has to think about satisfying the needs of the other two participants. We succeeded, I hope, because that was all we had in our minds.

It was gratifying. Our contentment was reflected in the fact that we overslept the next morning and I don't think we even realised the hour when we struggled into the kitchen to regain our strength with honey and yoghourt for breakfast. We exchanged glances, the three of us, like kids who had done something very naughty but were left feeling just great inside.

It felt so rebellious, so out of the ordinary, so terribly outrageous and the extraordinary thing was that instead of isolating my feelings for David, it brought me much closer to him because it was just something audacious that we could hold over everyone else.

It gave our love a special kind of blend so that we could get into other moments like that without injuring our feelings for one another. It was boosting to the mind and the body.

When we regained our composure and studied the clock, we could not believe that it was already 10.50. We had to be at Beckenham Register office for the ceremony by 11.00 a.m.

We just knew it was impossible but we scrambled into our wedding clothes and Clare got dressed and came with us as we piled into David's blue Fiat, for she was to be a witness.

We got to Beckenham at 11.30 and our guests, not to mention the Registrar and David's mother, were in a state of apoplexy.

"Sorry, everyone," mumbled David, "the traffic was dreadful out of London. We got caught in a jam."

The portly Registrar eyed us with relief.

The ceremony finally proceeded and the poor Registrar winced when he asked for the wedding ring to be produced.

We hadn't got one. But we had brought along four silver bracelets which my brother sent from Peru and we were going to exchange these.

David intended to wear two on his wrist and I would have the other pair. These, I explained to the perplexed Registrar, were to be our wedding bands in place of the traditional ring.

Our reception, like our honeymoon, was destined for Haddon Hall where our assortment of friends gathered in strength: David's musicians, Tony Visconti and his best pals George and Barry.

Celebrations, fuelled by casks of wine, were as uninhibited as the Greeks would make them, although we could only offer one table for guests to dance on and very little spare crockery to smash.

At the height of the revelry, David and I

crept stealthily away to our room, congratulating ourselves that we escaped unnoticed. We were exhausted.

Through the days leading up to our marriage David had consistently remarked: "I don't think I've ever made love so much since meeting you."

When we made love, everything was perfect. The feel, the touch, the tenderness . . . the sensitive act symbolising our love for one another.

And our love, when shared with others, gained yet another dimension, of the untried and the unknown, where we could make explorations in the realms of the Karma Sutra.

I always wanted to be the ultimate point of David's passions, but I realised in those first days of marriage that I had to adapt to the more practical role of being a wife, of keeping a home for him and putting down roots.

I worked hard to preserve that balance, knowing how important all those aspects were.

Haddon Hall was looking more snug; a friend intimated that it radiated the warmth of a curio shop and I suppose it did with antiques and secondhand furnishings vying for space with guitars, saxophones, ironing, board, television and art nouveau lampshades. Space was really at a premium in the living room when a grand piano came over from a neighbour opposite. David also bought me a fantastic peacock's tail fan to brighten our bedroom, into which was installed a couple of wardrobes and a dressing table.

We also had a big, old, carved-wood French four-poster Limoges bed, but it arrived a day or two late for the start of our honeymoon.

Our household designs might have been too outrageous and progressive for Ideal Home but they inspired so many things and one idea gave germ to David's album cover for "The Man Who Sold The World".

The living room walls and ceiling were painted hunting green and the lace curtains dyed scarlet.

David, a black beret on his head, was pictured in the room wearing a beautiful pseudo medieval dress, dealing a pack of art deco playing cards on to the floor. He looked at the camera with an expression of impending disaster.

It was a breathtaking album cover, but it was banned in America because it was considered to have homosexual connotations. In time we got used to this kind of hypocrisy.

Unlike other newly married couples we weren't going to be alone.

David's musicians, roadies and friends were congregated at our house.

Some of them lived in—rock bands were like that. They came as a pack, or not at all.

For better, for worse, we had lured this great band from Hull, originally known as The Rats, on the recommendation of their roadie Peter Hunsley, who was now one of our friends. They were down to back David.

Mick Ronson, a blond-haired boy who played lead guitar, was a brilliant instrumentalist whose early work was influenced by Jeff Beck but whose own style was soon to develop.

Ronno came from a dedicated Mormon family, but his religious convictions were now to be severely tested by the environmental hazards of the road.

The bass man, Trevor Bolder, was an amazing looking guy. He had long, beautiful black hair with deep, curly sideboards that could be sprayed, white, gold or crimson, to give him a dramatic appearance on stage.

Woody Woodmansey replaced David's original drummer John Cambridge and he possessed a natural talent that other musicians admired. In character, he was a nice all round guy. Drummers are a special breed. They are pretty solid and one could always rely on Woody. Strangely enough, he later became a Scientologist, which never ceased to amaze me.

Our other roadie was Roger Fry, an Aussie who was hard to get mobile and who finally got fired when he failed us on an important gig.

These, then, were Haddon Hall's "house guests" and as well as a husband to look after, I also had a family of "sons".

They all had to be clothed, fed and cared for. I couldn't make a special case of David and ignore the others.

My kitchen became like a transport cafe with a teapot constantly whistling on the stove and a couple of frying pans churning out bangers, baked beans, eggs and bacon to order!

Sliced bread would go through the toaster with the rapidity of a sten gun. I would cook a proper dinner in the evening.

Determined to make David's band the smartest in the land, I would preach to the boys about their day-to-day appearances.

"It's just as essential to look as handsome off-stage as it is on," I would say to them. "We're in the theatre. We've got to be glamorous in the very way we live our lives."

In the hall, because there wasn't any other room, the washing machine and spin dryer were going full pelt most days.

I would grab their soiled clothes while they slept and toss it all into the whirring machines.

I also did the ironing.

Thankfully, the band gave me a lot of help in the kitchen. They would all help with the washing up and clearing the dishes. They would also mend blown fuses and undertake other odd jobs. One or two of them would do gardening.

David turned the basement of the house into a studio with the assistance of Tony Visconti, whose father had taught him his trade as a carpenter before he became a record producer.

Tony, who doubled on bass guitar besides producing David's records, lived for a spell in our only spare bedroom with his girl friend Liz. Later he married the singer Mary Hopkin.

The outstanding memory I have of Haddon Hall is that we were never lost for friends!

The only place where I could exchange private thoughts with David was in our bedroom, but even then it wasn't always a sanctuary we could call our own!

Other musicians and thespians would invade us—our living room was like a convention assembly where all sorts of blueprints for fame were juggled. Enough ideas were tossed forward to change the world.

Songwriter Lionel Bart who masterminded the West End musical "Oliver!" was a great chum; so too was the actress-singer Dana Gillespie, and many of the kids who were still associated with the Arts Lab would turn up.

David would encourage them because he saw the ultimate talent that existed in them and I remember there was a boy called Brian Moore who used to make eight-foot-tall papier-mache puppets.

Our house was nothing but theatrical—drums rolling, guitars twanging in the rehearsal room, players on the verandah and lawn. It was a scenario of its own.

On stage David was seen as an extrovert, I think most entertainers are, but in private he was sensitive and shy, particularly with strangers and meeting someone for the first time.

But in his own environment at Haddon Hall he enjoyed being surrounded by friends he admired and those who respected him. His charm, wit and humour took a keen edge.

As an artist, David needed freedom and I tried to give him that, by accepting our bizarre way of life at Haddon Hall.

When David and the band began to arrange gigs the days became hectic, especially for our costume designer Freddie Buretti.

We threw together a tailor's shop with a sewing machine and ironing board, installed for the making and fittings of new, and what might be modestly termed extravagant, costumes!

Showbusiness is essentially glamour, and David was behind me in cultivating that theory generally among the boys. Every important gig and television appearance contracted by the group meant fresh outfits for them.

"It's no good the band going on stage in gold lame and diamante costumes if they're going to wear jeans out on the streets," I told David, "because they will spoil all the good they will have done."

So I asked Freddie to design the band's leisure clothes in subdued colours and muted tones in the character of their stage costumes, using only mohairs, silks and Cashmeres.

Poor Freddie didn't stop working. As soon as he finished one set of outfits some new gig or performance would be arranged and he would have to start cutting again.

His girl friend Daniella and I would also help, hand-sewing and pressing the new clothes, so would Mickey King and Darryl, friends of Freddie's. We were quite a little factory!

Stitching silk linings into costumes, turning cuffs and lapels, elasticating waistbands . . . Freddie would supervise it but we all became expert with needle and thread.

I had been married to David for seven months when to our joy and careful planning I became pregnant. David loved kids and he was always amazing with them.

We waited for quite a while but now I knew it was time to have a baby and give him something to be responsible for and to inspire him. I was petrified at the thought of having a baby, but I suppose that was only natural. At least I was young and I could get it over and done with.

Our aim was to have one child of our own and then adopt others. I have no doubt this was the influence we felt from David's father and his service to Dr. Barnardo's. There were too many unwanted children in the world and we had become very conscious of this problem.

My pregnancy left me feeling dreadful but the band were understanding and they treated me like a princess. They helped a great deal around the house and did anything requested of them.

Mick Ronson—known as "Ronno" in the family—would also assist in the kitchen. He loved to cook curried beans, but every time he did they would make me physically sick because I couldn't bear the smell.

Woody would prepare big pots of tea and in the days I was confined to bed he would lumber in and have a chat. We would talk about all the things that affected the band— the gigs they were doing, the albums and tours that were being arranged for the future.

In time, my condition improved, or maybe I had just become accustomed to it. My bouts of morning sickness were less frequent.

During my pregnancy David had to go on a three-week tour of America to promote his new album "The Man Who Sold The World".

I talked with him twice a week on the phone and I remember one call came through when I was poised 12 foot high up on a ladder, having decided to paint the ceiling of the spare bedroom!

"Why are you doing that?" cried David, panic stricken from the other side of the Atlantic, "you'll fall and kill yourself. Let the job wait till I get home."

"All right David," I assured him, "I'm sorry. I'll leave it alone. . . ."

Of course, I was determined to finish the ceiling as I wanted to have all the decorations complete for his return.

When David got back he was annoyed that I had not taken his advice, but relieved to think that there had been no mishap.

Indeed, the only mishap at this time occurred to David and it caused us the most terrible alarm.

David had two old Riley cars. He was always pottering around with them, stripping them down and reassembling them. It was one of his hobbies, but I don't think either of the cars was very reliable.

Going into London one afternoon he stalled outside Lewisham Police Station. When he couldn't restart the car, he attempted to crank it with the starting handle. Unfortunately, he left the car in gear and it jumped forward. The starting handle buried itself in David's leg, the wound almost reaching a main artery. He was rushed to hospital and was detained for nearly a week.

Poor David. He was still limping when he came home and we had to get a private doctor to re-examine his leg.

Like many expectant mothers, I had begun to fancy certain spices and foods.

I developed the most insatiable passion for Chinese food and often David drove into London to get me Peking duck and rice. Once in the middle of the night!

David was warming to his role of becoming a father. He was inspired to write a song he titled "Kooks"—about two kooky parents! The song found its way on to the "Hunky Dory" album.

With only a month before our baby was due, I was feeling superbly fit and I went out dancing with David to the Sombrero restaurant in London.

I really let my hair down and our friends said I looked like a piece of string with a knot tied in the middle. . . .

We wanted a son and I knew we would get one. We had already settled on his name. We would call him Zowie but give him two other Christian names.

We chose Duncan, purely because we liked the name, and we also named him Heywood after David's father.

In Greek the word "zoe" means life. In English it is also the spelling of a girl's name. So we adapted the name as Zowie, rhyming too with Bowie although this wasn't a deliberate gimmick.

Some people considered it was at the time and there was a danger that Zowie too might come to think this, but we thought he could always discard this name in preference for his other two Christian names whenever he wished.

Zowie, all eight pounds, eight ounces of him, came into the world with a jolt.

I cracked my pelvis in the delivery, which was an experience I did not think I could ever face again and the doctors in the Bromley Hospital annexe, where our child was born, must have thought of me as being the loudest patient to have come into their care during labour.

Barely out of hospital, I suffered from post natal depression. A midwife said it was normal and so did the doctor, but I could not get over it.

Every time Zowie yelled I panicked—I didn't know what to do. I just couldn't cope with him all of the time.

I became frightened—frightened of what I might do. I was full of nervous tension. I didn't know how to stop him crying. I'd feed him, change his nappy, rock him in his cot, cradle him in my arms, pat his back. But he would still cry and within days of being home I was on the verge of a breakdown.

One afternoon, as a respite from it all, I

went over to Dana's home in Kensington leaving Zowie to David and Roger.

I found Dana packing for a holiday in Italy.

"Why don't you come with me?" she said, when I told her how bananas I was getting with Zowie.

It was a crazy idea, but the more I thought about it, the better it sounded. So I called David and explained what I had in mind.

"Great. Why not?" he replied. "You need a break Angie. Don't worry, we'll look after Zowie."

I went home and packed. Within hours I was on my way to the airport to join Dana.

I handed Zowie over to the safe keeping of David, pointing out the basketful of disposable nappies ready for use!

I was confident that Zowie would be well looked after and I knew that Freddie's girl friend Daniella, responsible angel that she was, could be relied upon to help.

Zowie's bottle feed was simple to prepare and Daniella was already familiar with the routine.

It was as well that I couldn't breast feed Zowie or I would not have been able to go away. My chest was described as two fried eggs on a plate!

Reaching Italy with Dana, I tried to forget the whole ordeal I had come through, but I'm afraid it was impossible.

It was as if my body had gone through a chemical change. The instincts of motherhood could not be obliterated by the warm Adriatic sunshine.

Should I have really entertained the idea of a bachelor-girl holiday and left my infant behind in England?

58

Unsettled days would culminate in a call home at nights to ensure that Zowie was safe and well.

It was great to get home but the holiday had been valuable from one particular aspect—that now I was ready to undertake my responsibility in the way I should have done from the beginning.

David and the boys in the band had been amazing. They had handled Zowie with expertise. Bottle-feeds, changing nappies, tucking Zowie down to sleep, were orchestrated like their music.

My absence had also created a special communication between David and his son which might not have materialised otherwise. I always thought that having a child would be good for David inasmuch that it would be a stabilising influence on him.

It would make him think of home as something more than just a base.

Artists need to feel affection. Their morale, their egos search for it. But by the same token, they also need roots and a home simply isn't one without children.

David acknowledged this gladly. The homestead and what it meant to him, provided a perfect antidote to the mounting pressures of his career.

We were fortunate. There were few squabbles between us and if anything, I think I was always the more dramatic.

I regarded planet Earth as a theatre and I would exploit its stage, even when it boiled down to mundane, domestic issues.

Once I was having an argument with David—one of the household bills was at question—when he dismissed my diatribe in an instant.

"I can't stand this B-movie dialogue any longer," he said.

I thought about it and I had to admit he was right.

I was never afraid of telling David what I thought, but maybe I didn't need to deliver such rhetoric in making a simple point.

David would rarely fight back. He pursued the line of peace at all costs.

There was only one real tiff that I can recall where things got out of hand.

Throwing a fit of pique because David was late for dinner one night, I slunk to bed on my own and locked the bedroom door behind me.

David started hammering the door and yelling: "Angie let me in, do you hear?"

I didn't budge.

But I didn't count on David breaking the door down! Buffeting it open with his shoulder he flew into the room and he was crimson with rage.

"Never lock me out of the bedroom again," he snapped.

I had never seen that kind of aggression in him before. His nature was always so gentle.

As a husband he had so many fine qualities. He was very generous, very talented and very respected in his field of endeavour. What more could a wife ask for?

Shopping was mainly my concern and at Christmas time I would divide the presents into three piles and say, "These are from you to me, here are mine to you and these are ours to Zowie."

When David was abroad he always brought me back great, funny presents—a red lacquered and mirrored musical box from Madeira with a pink tutu ballet dancer who popped up from the box and spun round.

From Russia he brought a beautiful lacquered jewellery box. David had a wonderful way of finding the ethnic identity of people and buying souvenirs which reminded one of that.

In another class of gift, he gave me the most beautiful things—a necklace of seed pearls and later in our marriage I acquired two mink coats, one a gorgeous white creation with black fox collar and sleeves.

David and I got a mink coat for his mother too, to cheer her up. We also sent her on holiday to Cyprus and we took her on various outings like the Ideal Home exhibition.

We bought a fur coat too for Marion Skene, the Scottish nanny we employed to look after Zowie and we got another fur-lined coat for Daniella.

Even when we were more financially secure, I made it a rule to try and not pay more than a hundred pounds a dress, unless it was something very special.

While David's stage costumes were extravagant, his clothes around the house were simple and casual. Because he liked to paint and use oils, he would sometimes wear a smock so that if he accidentally spilt something, it wouldn't matter. A set of his expressionist pictures were reproduced in Time magazine many years later.

He was as talented as an expressionist artist as he was a wonderful, dynamic live performer or recorded songwriter—my husband's talent seemed limitless and I realised he was a fine renaissance figure in the scope and application of his creativity.

David's smock, or a variation of it, caused raised eyebrows when my husband described it to a journalist as a "man's dress" which in time was to have its own connotations although we did not realise it then.

I would buy a lot of David's clothes but when it came to presents he was very easy to please. He always loved art books and albums by other musicians.

I also bought him a golden tenor saxophone for his birthday. I would marvel at David's ability not only to play sax, but to play the piano and guitar, although at that time he wasn't able to read a note of music.

David admired many other writers—the Beatles, Mick Jagger and Keith Richards among them, but more especially Tony Newley, who not only influenced David's writing at this period, but also his performances and persona on stage, the voice catching much of Newley's phrasing and intonation.

But David could never be an imitator. He would often pay token tribute to another artist he admired, but essentially he had to be original.

Many of his compositions he offered to others to record before contemplating his own interests.

I remember he wrote "All The Young Dudes" for Mott the Hoople and gave "Oh You Pretty Things" to Peter Noone to record.

David's career was going well. Very well.

4

Seeking to get closer to heaven,
Closer to heaven than my song.

David was responsible for the creativity and output of so many people: that is one of the joys of being a star.

People would start to ring him early in the morning and their calls would continue all day while the band rehearsed and David sang, wrote or conducted business.

Daniella and Freddie would sew in the next room and I would keep house, performing the household duties, and advising David in certain areas.

Gradually David became dissatisfied with his manager Ken Pitt. They had grown apart in understanding the direction in which David wanted to grow. This was very unfortunate as Ken had contributed and collaborated in David's earlier dreams and aspirations, before these gelled into the embryonic form of "The Man Who Sold The World" and "Ziggy Stardust".

It was hard for everyone. I know that Tony Visconti felt that David was spending far too much time at home, planning and consulting with me and Freddie and the boys. He missed having the opportunity to discuss their projected plans.

But in all I think we knew this was a period of birth and creativity. David was entering an artistic cycle that would come full circle in terms of performance, gratification and sales volume for RCA's profit margin.

The reason we had suddenly become aware of sales profit margins was the arrival in our midst of Tony DeFries, a 30-year-old wheeler-dealer from the East End of London, who helped David secure a release from Ken Pitt.

My fondest early memory of spending time with Tony was when David was asked to do the Glastonbury Fayre. Tony, Dana Gillespie and myself watched one of David's most spectacular performances as dawn broke over the Somerset countryside. He was playing alone without a backing band and even today people still write to me about it.

Tony was developing and showing new talents and at this event he took over the details of the minute-to-minute timing of a live performance. It was fascinating to watch him ease into this new role. He had no trouble in adopting the theatrical and musical mode of operation and making it more streamlined and efficient.

Tony, who affectionately became known as Tony DeFreak among us, had set out in life as a solicitor's clerk.

His legal knowledge was sufficient to deal with contractual and legal papers affecting David's career.

For some reason he always looked on us as a couple of urchins who needed a helping hand. We developed an affection for him and he for us. It didn't seem like a business relationship.

Tony took care of everything for us. Whenever one of our artistic friends was in trouble, we'd drag Tony into the arena to try and help them.

Tony was unafraid. He would always go in at the deep end without so much as batting an eyelid.

Lionel Bart's case was a classic one. His financial affairs were in a state of catastrophe. No-one had been able to sort him out.

But Tony waded in and after all sorts of manipulations advised Lionel to declare himself bankrupt. In the public's eye that made Lionel some sort of hero, because we all love a man who has got the courage to say where he is at.

On hindsight Lionel wasn't so sure. Not being able to sign a cheque, or open an account, he had not foreseen all the consequences and until he successfully applied for his discharge, he still wasn't sure that he had accepted the right advice. But Tony knew that there had been only one way he could have directed him and today I think Lionel knows that.

Tony also assisted Dana Gillespie with a spate of problems she ran into and next he was thrashing out the lives of our musicians.

In the early days at Haddon Hall we were invariably short of money. David would give me housekeeping, and the boys would chip in, but we were always on the knife edge.

Record royalties were slow filtering through.

Unpaid household bills mounted, but they always got paid in the end.

When the band needed new clothes I would hire a mini cab to take me into London to do the shopping. As I didn't drive myself it was the most practical thing to do.

We would send out flowers to musicians of other contemporary bands, struggling for success as we were at the time, so that at least we would attach some significance to opening nights.

Good times, luckily, were around the corner and Tony DeFries's new contract deals began to pump through fresh funds.

David was a prodigious songwriter, but like so many other creative talents, the process did not always come easily for him.

The gestation of an album was always a very depressing period.

He would get the blues until he had scored at least eight songs and then, seeing light at the end of the tunnel, he would sail through the other three or four remaining tracks to complete an album.

Many music critics felt I influenced David's writing, but it was a romantic notion that made good copy. Certainly, I contributed opinions and suggestions that any normal wife would do and sometimes I would recognise odd lines in his lyrics that might have stemmed from our conversations, but nothing more. They were all David's songs, born of his own hard labours.

David had come a long way from early days of the sixties, which he would recount to me. Sometimes the expression on his face would be one of humour, other times, it would reflect only his past frustrations.

David was born in Brixton in 1947 and was brought up in a four-roomed house in a street where the neighbours were predominantly Irish and Jamaican. David had a step-brother Terry and a step-sister who later got married and went to Egypt.

His life was difficult and David didn't always get on with his mother. When he was 13 or 14 he was injured in a school fight and nearly lost the sight of his left eye. This explained why the pupil of David's left eye was larger than that of the right and quite often he wore a patch over the eye whenever it felt tired or ached.

One of David's teachers at Bromley Arts School was Peter Frampton's father and Peter was one of the kids who followed David's career.

After college David worked as a junior visualiser with an advertising agency for six months, but having learned to play the saxophone as a boy he was also playing with local rhythm and blues groups in Bromley, as he had since early school days.

Later, he became a Buddhist and very nearly entered a monastery in Scotland.

"It would have meant total commitment," David told me.

But from the teachings of the monks he adopted many simple philosophies on life. David had an anathema about looking back on past events. Buddhism had taught him only to look forward, to consider and plan the future. What happened yesterday, was past.

David turned back to music and returned to London. He was playing in the Marquee Club and it was there that Ken Pitt spotted him.

David's first band was named Davie Jones and the King Bees. Their hopes of instant fame were quickly dashed. Their one single, "Liza Jane", didn't do that well.

Next, David sang with another group, The Mannish Boys, whose music, similar to The Who's, was loud and very angry.

In 1966 The Monkees came in on a massive publicity campaign and a namesake of David's was one of the adulated quartet.

David, not wishing to be confused with anyone else, preserved individuality by adopting the name of "Bowie" after the knife. David performed with yet another band, The Lower Third, and then put out two singles of his own, "Do Anything You Say" and "I Dig Everything".

When David switched labels from Pye to Deram, and there was a later spell with Pye, he was hailed as something of a social commentator when one of his singles, "The London Boys" related the attempts of two teenagers to become hip. It was the time when there was a running fracas between two factions of teenagers in Britain, the Mods and Rockers.

By the time I became married to David he had toured with Feathers, but he had not yet cut his "Space Oddity" album. This was inspired by the movie "2001" which, he told me, captivated him.

There was an ironic twist. The title song, which won an Ivor Novello award for him, and which recreated the loneliness of a stranded astronaut, was played as a theme song to the televised showing of the Moon landing by Neil Armstrong.

Realising the necessity to play to live audiences, David embarked on a string of British tours and even opened on gigs for Peter Frampton's Humble Pie and David Edmunds' Love Sculpture and he once appeared as a special guest doing mime supporting Marc Bolan's cosmic folk band Tyrannosaurus Rex.

As distinct from other rock 'n' roll musicians, David was a pioneer. He pioneered rock 'n' roll theatre—to him every stage presentation had to be theatrically implemented.

Having studied mime and make-up with Lindsay Kemp, a well known theatrical instructor, his whole concept for the stage was so different from any other band.

Costume, lights, and theme were key factors for him. He created a spate of fictional characters. But this was much later on.

These were still the early days. Struggling, hell-for-leather days when we had to establish David as a star.

Sometimes it felt like going to war and I wasn't going to be left out of the action. I was an unofficial "roadie" and I had to be prepared for combat.

We played some pretty wild gigs. Beer cans showered the stage at a Gravesend club, where a mob of young dockers grew impatient to boogie with their girl friends and they were determined not to give David a fair hearing.

I saw things were going to get rough as I mingled with the audience out front. One heckler in a tapered Mod suit and string tie threw his lit cigarette straight at David's face but luckily missed him.

I moved over to the youth and kneed him hard in the groin. His face contorted with pain and fighting broke out as he attempted to grab hold of me. Suddenly, I was grappling with two policemen who were on the verge of arresting me before I could persuade them amid the commotion that I had not instigated the trouble.

We travelled to gigs in the Fiat 500 that David had inherited from his father and I remember once we were travelling up to Birmingham when the strong cross wind caught the two speakers we had tied on to the roof. Our little car blew right across the M1, almost like a sail plane, but we escaped without injury or accident.

We persevered and with the arrival of the band from Hull the boys did their first gig at the Roundhouse in London where Marc Bolan and Jeff Dexter—the dee-jay of the day—watched the action with care.

David's popularity was widening and it was reflected in a posse of fans who kept vigil at Haddon Hall.

At the outset I made pots of tea for the fans and fed them cakes.

They were really nice. They were all teenagers and they didn't want anything apart from the chance maybe to talk to David or Ronno or to get an autograph.

Alternatively, they would just chat to me and make a splendid fuss of Zowie.

The fans, who would carve their initials on the bricks outside the front door or on the bark of the trees on the driveway, wanted to feel part of something.

They sensed that David was going to be a star and transmitted these feelings to me. They wanted to know simple things, like how we lived, what David said and did. They had wanted to feel an empathy with us.

This kind of climate grew with David's success and soon there were lots of fans outside our gates. It became, sadly, impossible to cope with them all.

Our house was no longer a home. We had no privacy. To get out of the drive, we had to run a gauntlet of teenagers.

Secretly, we made plans to move out of Haddon Hall. It was going to be a wrench, but there was nothing else we could do.

The band found a self-contained flat of their own. David, Zowie and I took an apartment in Maida Vale that belonged to actress Diana Rigg.

Six months later we were on the move again, this time to Oakley Street in Chelsea where we rented a four-bedroom Regency town house.

Freddie and Daniella came along with us and occupied the basement. It was good to have at least two of our friends with us.

In the meantime, David and Tony had also established an office at Gunter Grove and had launched their own company, Mainman.

There was promise in the air.

I kept in close touch with my parents.

When Zowie was six months old we holidayed in Cyprus with them and visited Lefkara, where the finest Cypriot lace is made. We bought several yards of it for the new house.

We spent a second holiday in Cyprus with Woody and Ronno and got into a lot of fresh adventures. We crashed in our hired car at fork roads just outside Kyrenia and David, who was driving, was accused of careless driving but the case against him was dismissed when it was discovered that no "right of way" signs were erected at the spot.

David got along with my parents very well. To him they were like two friends, Helen and George.

My father tried to advise David on financial matters. He was appalled by David's revelations of how pop groups were constantly being ripped off by unscrupulous managers and promoters.

"Whatever happens, you mustn't let it happen to you. There must be ways to protect your interests," my father told him.

We had to forgive my father for his optimism. David was to become a victim like everybody else.

It's a penalty of superstardom. We had to learn to live with it and cope with it.

5

Touch and Tell, we tried to touch with music's love
We tried to tell with theatre's ironic dove

Light is clear casts off disguises
Light pierces darkness, truth surprises
Light is gifted to a million faces
You cannot catch or colour its secret choice or places.

I will not crutch my shattered dreams and hopes
Rolling old religions up dangerous rocky slopes,
I cannot pray and thus possess
Power and success are hateful to godliness.

I can but try to Touch and Tell
Judging which is heaven and which is hell
Heaven is the mainstream conscious thought
And hell's cages are the goods and fame I bought
Infinity, come back for us we are so near

David was being David. He was being honest. When a Melody Maker reporter asked him if he was gay he replied, "Yes, I am."

My husband could not have possibly envisaged the impact his simple statement was to have on public opinion.

Social ethics and structures started to change. Gay people breathed more easily, without fear of recrimination.

Newspapers and magazines took up the theme. People were actually speaking about a subject that in the past had remained strictly taboo.

Naturally, I was asked to express my opinion. Was I shocked by David's admission?

I wasn't going to back pedal. Not now. "We are both free spirits," I said.

We decided to make a stand on the subject as a matter of policy.

Gay people came to thank us personally for the exposure we gave to the subject.

They were no longer afraid, they said, although unfortunately I wish this had been true in more cases.

At least they could now express their own feelings and their experiences without the stigma they once believed would be attached to such admissions.

David was casually surprised by the sequence of events.

"Angie," he whispered one night, "what's happening?"

"I don't know," I said, but then thought about it. There was an answer, but I had to ponder a while.

"Things have been needing a change. Times, places and people are speeding up and to cope with this evolutionary paranoia strange people are chosen who through their art can move progress more quickly," I said.

It was the most stimulating and reflective period of our marriage.

This time we were putting our concepts on trial.

We were under the microscope.

Some people strongly attacked our views as "too outrageous to even contemplate". Church and moral welfare societies rapped us for our indiscreet statements.

One of our own profession, Cliff Richard, blamed us for the disintegration of the moral fibre of society.

I guess that Cliff, like one or two other people, was scared that the world was getting tighter and that truth would finally have to be defined and faced up to.

From the enormous volume of letters we got from all parts of the world, I reasoned that our efforts had not been in vain.

Others wrote to us with their problems, feeling that we might hold the solution for them.

Suddenly, I found myself playing "Dear Marje", answering all sorts of letters, sometimes where a family crisis was at stake.

There were letters from couples where one or the other partner had become involved in a gay experience which they felt would threaten their happiness.

I would put forward my beliefs. The same beliefs I hold today. Why should bisexuality be the cause for the breakdown of a perfectly healthy marriage because at some stage in one's life you want to experience something different?

I tried to answer all of the letters as honestly and as constructively as I could.

75

David would get letters from girls and boys pledging their undying love for him.

Through all of this, I came to know an amazing variety of people and somehow they all had something to say and to teach.

I loved to be able to observe people's interchanges in the course of social conversation. I enjoyed blending different types of people so they might get to know one another and understand one another better.

I think we all learned a lot about attitudes, thought patterns and conscious reflexes borne of ethnic conditioning.

I guess from it all I felt most sympathy with those who emerged as transvestites.

They gravitated to show business, because show business gave them an area of acceptance which they sought. They found a haven where they could work without ridicule or stigma.

We were given credit for something very deep.

In terms of David's career, all this interest and controversy had no ill effects. Somehow each single release, each album, each tour seemed to be an event for those who had no banner to wave. But they could all be sheltered under the umbrella of Bowie's music.

He touched on all facets of life—sexuality, the mystical, the physicality of being and the mental effort required to find a satisfactory solution to the question of life.

New audiences flocked to David, his style and theatrical mood inspiring a new awareness. They found an identity with him. He gained new allies who appreciated what he was doing.

There was some reticence to begin with in

America, but slowly the message got through.

David rose to his followers. He wrote liberated songs and they loved him for it!

In today's world, gay people can state their case. Whether anyone will listen is another matter, but at least the shackles now no longer confine you so totally. The handcuffs and leg irons allow you to stand and say, "Yes, Your Honour", and by God isn't that a change for the better?!

They don't even brand our arms or legs any more! Gay people now have their own societies and organisations, their own night clubs and even their own politics. They've got something of everything. Unfortunately, as with everything in the inflated 1980's world, there is a price.

You buy your gay freedom. I don't need to underline this fact more than I already have. Prejudice is not dead.

A friend of mine recently asked me if I thought Zowie would ever come to condemn David or me for our admission of being bisexual.

I replied, "No, I hope not. It was the truth and it was right to speak up at that time. There was no intention of embarrassing him or harnessing with him a burden greater than he could assume. The intention was always to let him know the predominant truth. That the truth must prevail is inherently right in every aspect of life.

"I hope my son will turn out to be a fine and understanding person. I hope one day that he will even be able to admire the principles I hold dear. If on the other hand he finds it unacceptable then I'll presume that he has a higher order of life in mind

77

and will join a monastery." My friend nodded assent.

I guess it is always a question of choice. A man must choose whatever in life makes him content and so it is for parents and for children.

Neither one has a greater need for their identity to be unique and sacred. The passage of time is the only judge of the merit and worth of a man. Who remembers him? Who makes him come alive with conversation many generations later? That is the merit of a man wealthy in soul.

6

He met a little redhead who could sing and sing and sing

Suddenly David's career took off. "Ziggy Stardust" was a huge success. The release of this incredible album was accompanied by a live performance tour with full record company backing.

Everything was promoted. The cover, the billboards of David up and down the country. Constant air play on the radio stations. Reviews and editorial in all the papers.

"Ziggy Stardust" was toured as an album, not as a concept. Therefore his band, named The Spiders From Mars, were on stage with him all the time during this show and David was the one who dropped in and out of songs vocally and instrumentally, giving them scope to improvise over and above their own solo spots.

Ronno would lean back with that haunting, wailing guitar to accompany him, looking like a young Greek god. They were all terrific. What exciting times! And crowds. Crowds of people everywhere. In hotel lobbies, behind stage doors. Every concert hall sold out up and down the country. In Europe and in America.

David and the boys seemed calm, but were inwardly excited. They knew they could do it and were getting set to take on the onslaught.

David's "aliens in our midst" theme was personified in Ziggy, a rock 'n' roll singer whose ego motivates his downfall at the hands of his own musicians, the Spiders from Mars.

It was a role which gave David scope to exploit theatrical drama to its limitations in a rock 'n' roll context.

Ziggy was given an identity by Freddie who created a glittering array of costumes and by

Suzy Fussey who fashioned a hair style from photographs David showed her. So Ziggy was born. A fantasy figure into which David became totally immersed.

His hair was dyed bright red and blown dry into a perfect-looking puff ball, razor trimmed to the sideboards. He wore the traditional Ziggy suit, tight sculptured trousers tucked into high lacing boots with a short cinch waist jacket, tight to the body with shirt-style sleeves—in all colours, in all fabrics. David and the boys wore these costumes on stage and their fans copied them, arriving at shows sporting these wonderful creations.

Strangely enough, I received my greatest compliment at this time. Tony DeFries noticed that many of the girl fans at the concerts were copying the way I dressed.

Said Tony one night, "We've got seven or eight Angies sitting out in the audience. . . ."

I was astounded. And so was David. I caught sight of one girl. A platinum haired teenager who was very pretty and had got herself a dark green woollen dress like the one I had been seen out in only a week before. She wore stiletto heels in the same colour. Even her hair style and make up were identical to my look.

Two or three weeks after this, Tony called me and asked me if I wanted to do a photosession for a London national newspaper, The Sun. He said he had been mulling over the phenomenon of so many girls at a Bowie gig dressing as I did that he thought it was time for me to get a chance to express my fashion flair. It all seemed so complimentary.

I loved this whole period of time. I felt gratified to be able to contribute any sort of activity which would create exposure for David and the band.

Their music was explosive on the Ziggy tour. It had a beginning, a middle and an end. At the outset it was the ominous warning of "five years, that's all we've got" and then the scene switched to "Suffragette City" where the action was "wham bam, thank you ma'am" and culminated in "Rock 'n' Roll Suicide" a vision of life at the end of a broken rainbow.

One critic who reviewed the show wrote, "At the end of the performance Bowie called out to his audience, 'You're wonderful, give me your hands.' I was expecting to see cripples run and loaves of bread and fish multiply."

I suppose that was the impression.

Even at home David would reflect his stage persona in his daily living habits. In his moods, conversation and clothes.

It was like being married to a different man. And he adopted another identity during the time of "Aladdin Sane", a superstar trying to cope with the stresses of overnight fame.

David's concepts always reflected his deepest psychological convictions—mostly autobiographical. I think I could see that more than anyone, because I recognised some of our experiences and could imagine more from earlier times that he told me about.

Everyone of his albums had a different theme, with the exception, that is, of "Pin Ups", which was a glossary of the music of the Sixties. David and Twiggy were photographed by Justin de Villeneuve for the cover.

My hair was cut short like Twiggy's at the

time and I think some people mistakenly believed it was me on the sleeve with David.

David and I were often described as "look-alikes", although we didn't see it ourselves.

Through those years our lives changed considerably, although I doubt if either of us saw the signals, as fame allowed us precious little breathing space.

David and the band were now the property of their audience. They had to be seen.

They had to be out on the road and when I went with them we had to make our home wherever we travelled.

We were like a circus with an entourage of thirty, comprising musicians, roadies, engineers and technical crew, secretaries, wardrobe assistants and hair stylists.

It may have been considered strange for me to have gone on the road at all, but that is how David and I started together.

He performing and I providing the back-up, rather like a stage manager.

Life was hard and a little bleak on the road, and after the first tour, David never approved of me being there, especially working.

He preferred to have Zowie and me tucked up at home and joining him occasionally to see the special and important shows on each tour.

He toured America, Europe, Japan and the Far East, covering thousands of miles in the process.

But David, fascinated by the Space Age, was a jet-setter without getting into an aeroplane! By his own admission, he was scared stiff of flying. One turbulent flight from Cyprus was enough to convince him that he could get killed.

His travel was restricted to boats, trains

and cars and I remember going to America with him in some style enjoying the luxury of the QE2 for the Atlantic crossing.

There were times, of course, when the only passenger ships out of port were freighters—cargo ships with minimal passenger quarters and the smallest of berths.

Fortunately, good train services linked Europe.

David, on his way back from Japan, travelled through Russia on the romantic Trans-Siberian Express with Geoff McCormack, backing singer and dancer of "Diamond Dogs" show fame, and Bob Musel, my good friend from UPI and game journalist to boot.

We stayed in some great hotels.

Usually we had two suites, one for myself, Zowie and Marion and the other for David's use and entertaining guests.

Life on the road becomes an improvisation with a rock 'n' roll band. Living out of a suitcase makes it so. Luggage, travel tickets, passports, laundry, costumes and meals, as well as the concert schedules, all needed organising.

Some hotels barred rock 'n' roll groups from staying. I'm afraid The Who's tough reputation for smashing up places had travelled far and wide.

We were never kicked out of a hotel, but one or two made it clear that we wouldn't be welcome if we returned.

The only ban we did face was from the Beverly Wilshire hotel in Los Angeles where Tony disputed a 30,000 dollar bill.

Tony blamed me for it, but as I pointed out to him it was unlikely that I had gone through that amount of liquor and food on my own! The bill was finally paid.

There were all sorts of pitfalls on the road. Alcohol and drugs were just two of the hazards that many earlier touring musicians had warned us to be cautious of.

We ran into these kind of elements all over America but we were unresponsive.

We were geared to one objective—to make David's career happen once and for all. We were determined not to be sidetracked, not at this point.

I think we gained a lot of respect from our American promoters for that kind of deliberation and discipline.

The American fans might have thought they had got the gauge of British groups, having seen the Beatles, the Rolling Stones and The Who.

But they were unprepared for David, whose theatrical stage presentations were totally new to them. The reaction was electrifying.

"Ziggy", especially, bounced everybody around.

David's songs were analysed, like the decoding of a cypher. There had to be a meaning, a definition, to every word and line.

Love for a tough cookie was the theme of "Queen Bitch" and an undefined nymphet figures in "The Width of a Circle", while the general concensus was that another track, "Lady Stardust", was biographical because it was about an androgynous performer who resembled Bowie. I heard several other opinions, but it is all irrelevant to the music we are discussing.

Critics were something else. I could easily have socked a few of them but David would say, "Don't bother."

Some of the notices were interesting, like the one that read, "More than a sex symbol

Bowie is a clown, a sexless, faceless figure whose songs present a view of the world that is despairing and apocalyptic." Personally I think this is a great review of a fine and focussed performing artist.

Other critics objected to the way, they said, David performed simulated sex with Ronno's guitar during the act. Simulated sex? It was no such thing. David was attacking the guitar with his teeth. I imagine those same critics must have enjoyed reviewing blue movies.

David said in an interview: "I'm not particularly taken with life. I'd probably be very good as an astral spirit. I'm just a cosmic yob."

Sometimes, the fans would succeed in breaking through the cordons and they would seize pieces of David's costumes which he tauntingly held aloft. They tore jackets to shreds to keep as souvenirs.

Once I saw him standing bereft of everything except for the red jock strap he wore beneath his trousers. There was one last jewel pinned to the jock strap, hardly veiling David's anatomy!

Thirty pairs of trousers and as many jackets were needed at the start of David's tours and sometimes even this amount would not be enough. Shirts were lost by the hundred.

The fans would take everything they could.

David's pair of Peruvian wedding bands, which he wore on his wrists, were often taken from him but when the fans realised their significance, they were returned.

Then they disappeared permanently, and David got copies made of them from mine.

No-one worked harder on the road than David. Off stage he was still the leader, the hub of the industry around him. On stage he was the perfectionist in everything he did. Every song he performed required utmost precision and concentration from him.

He would lose about 2 lbs. in weight for every stage appearance he made and at the end of a tour he would look emaciated.

I cooked nutritious foods for him to regain his energy and proper weight which was around 145 lbs.

He would hardly get fit again before he was starting a fresh tour. He and the band could always count on another pattern of bizarre experiences—as I found when I flew out to join them in Japan.

Here, the trouble came from the Japanese habit of saying "Yes", parrot-fashion, when asked a question. Maybe they do not understand what is being asked of them and only answer "Yes" as a matter of politeness.

In a stadium holding more than 20,000 screaming fans, it was felt necessary from a security aspect to ensure that David and the band made their exit in a bus which was to be brought into a wire cage flanking the stage door.

But as the concert neared its end, and the encores grew deafening in volume, there was still no sign of the bus.

Things got a shade frantic.

Tony buttonholed the Japanese promoter, an amiable little fellow with a thatch of jet black hair and dark brown eyes.

"The bus? Where is it?" he asked.

"Yes," the promoter nodded graciously.

"Yes, but where?" cried Tony with exasperation ringing in his voice.

"Yes," he nodded again, "it is coming . . ."

"Ah, it's coming?"

"Yes," he said once more.

"But when?"

"Yes."

The bus did come, but far too late to avoid the seige of the fans on the dressing room door. David and the band were trapped for hours before making their escape.

In Tokyo the fans erupted with hysteria and invaded the stage. Seats in the auditorium collapsed with teenagers trapped beneath.

Scores of armed Japanese security guards moved in to break up the riot and it was terrifying.

Youngsters, many of them not involved in the riot, were hurled to the ground by the guards.

We didn't stand by and watch. I saw how badly the kids were crushed beneath the broken seats, which lay overturned in attached rows.

I strode forward and talked to one of the Japanese guards and said: "Let the kids through, because can't you see the others are getting hurt?" He didn't understand and held fast.

I called to our tour manager, Tony Zenetta, and Lee Blackchilders, the official tour photographer, but they couldn't hear a word through the din. So I weighed through the crowd and grabbed hold of them to come with me.

Our appearance caused a riot among the Japanese security men. They thought we were "heavies".

A melee ensued and I was eventually led to the safety of backstage by Stuey, David's personal bodyguard.

When peace was finally restored the hydraulic system of the stage had been ruined.

Pierre la Roche, Terry O'Neill and my leg.
Session arranged by Jean Dobson.

Angie at home, 1973.

Paris, 1973, on David's return from Russia. Photo by Barrie Wentzell.

"Who is that lumberjack?"

Dinner in Japan, April 1973. Photo by M. Sikita.

Off to Paris at 7am to record Pin-Ups. ."It's so early and I love you." Photo by Barrie Wentzell.

Paris collection, 1972.

Mummy and Zowie.

The Thin White Duke. David on stage.

At Dior. Paris 1972.

Photo by Terry O'Neill I

1978 Yuki collection. Photo by Terry O'Neill.

Top left: 1977. Photo by Terry O'Neill.

Left: Angie in Yuki for 1978 Hospital Charity fashion show.

As Carmen Miranda from the unproduced show, "Razor", written by Angie. Design by Regin, photo by Terry O'Neill.

Also from "Razor".

As Undine the water nymph.

Ruth Ellis. Design by gin, photo by Terry O'Neill.

As Prince Hildebrand from "Undine", 1973. "Good looking guy, huh?"

As Wonderwoman. Created by Terry O'Neill, Natasha Kornilof and Christine Mitchell-Driver at Mane Line's Savile Row salon 36 hours before flying to Hollywood for the NBC screentest.

Left: Live at Webbington Country Club. Right: With Roy Martin and Connie Constanzia live from Krisis Kabaret, the Little Theatre, Upper St Martins Lane.

With Dolly Parton.

Krisis Kabaret. Soul House cast.

*With fans at the premiere of
"The Man Who Fell to Earth".*

With Roy Martin.

With Drew Blood, Hollywood 1979.

Japan and the Orient brought a lot of influence into David's life. He was already involved with the Kabuki Theatre, the country's traditional theatre, and sometimes wore kimonos and costumes designed by Kansai Yamamoto, a wonderful friend. He and his wife and daughter made our stay in Japan all the more pleasant and exciting.

David wore some of the Japanese costumes in London at the start of the "Aladdin Sane" tour and the French make-up artist Pierre la Roche painted a gold sun on his forehead and lacquered his lips gold and his fingers scarlet.

We started another tour in America. Another riot occurred. We reached Detroit, a city that has real style. The kids looked slick and they poured to the theatre in limousines, bumper to bumper.

I could feel the energy building in the auditorium even before the concert began and it was ready to ignite when David and the band appeared.

The kids rushed the stage like a huge wave smacking down on the beach but they were repelled by a cordon of privately-hired security men in brown uniforms.

When I saw one of the security men punch a defenceless girl right in the face, I flew from my seat to intervene. He spun round and started choking me with both hands. I gasped for breath. My head began swimming.

Lee Blackchilders spotted my plight and thrashed his way through the crowd to come to my rescue. He grabbed hold of the security man and broke his grip on me.

I just kept prodding my neck to satisfy myself that it wasn't broken.

One of the roadies who had seen the incident from the wings said: "Lee saved your life Angie. I'm sure that guy would have killed you. . . . He was that mad."

Stresses and strains on a tour mount interminably and no one felt them more than David.

The pressures also stretched patience and tempers. By and large we were a pretty happy integrated family, but we could not always avoid squabbles.

If it was an argument over finance then I would leave it to Tony deFries to resolve but when there were other issues to settle then sometimes I would help.

David tried to stay out of all these petty squabbles which occurred on the road. He would rather leave things to Tony.

Life on the road was never without incident.

Much earlier we did a show at London's Rainbow Theatre with Bryan Ferry and Roxy Music who were playing as our supporting act.

It was normal procedure for our crew to check the sound before David and the band appeared. But Roxy Music had not finished their rehearsal, so it was impossible to make the check.

We had a conference and one of the roadies asked Roxy if we could conduct our sound check and if they would wind up their rehearsal.

They stopped playing and put down their instruments—and I suspect they blamed me for the abrupt end of their rehearsal.

It was rather funny because a year or two later, when Roxy were doing very well, I met them again and looked embarrassed. Bryan laughed as we recalled the incident. He said: "You are forgiven!"

We always had fond memories of the Rainbow. We did a Christmas Show there and asked guests to bring toys for Barnado's Homes. We were able to deliver a great truckload of presents to the children the next day. I'm sure David's father would have been proud of him.

David had achieved notoriety. Celebrities and stars made his opening nights of any new tour like gala occasions.

Rod Stewart, Elton John, the Beatles and the Rolling Stones were now familiar faces to David and in America he would find the Hollywood set attending his performances —Barbra Streisand, Jack Nicholson, Warren Beatty, Diana Ross and many others.

I didn't have to go through all of this. I guess people knew that I was difficult to deceive. I didn't need that kind of glamour, but I recognised it was good for David.

That, I hope, explains why I wasn't always there.

David, with another change of image, became the "Thin White Duke" wearing a wide brimmed trilby hat and a respectable suit.

Now and then a new face would be among us.

One new recruit was Tony Mascia who eventually became David's personal driver and bodyguard.

I found Tony in New York when I called for a car to take me to a restaurant. Tony was a 20-stone man with a good, strong, Italian face.

I told him to take me to Greenwich Village where the restaurant was situated.

Half an hour later we still hadn't got there. We'd lost our way.

In a New York accent he said: "I'm sorry ma'am, but this is my first day on the job. I'm from the Bronx and I don't know this side of town."

I sighed with exasperation.

"Well, why didn't you say so?" I said, "here, they must have given you a street guide. Let me have it and I'll direct you there."

I flicked over the pages and navigated him to the restaurant.

When I called the limo service the next day, I prevailed on them to send me a driver who knew his way about town.

Tony turned up.

"Sorry ma'am," he apologised, "I know just how you feel, but I'm the only guy they've got on duty."

Tony had been a truck driver and suffered a back injury that prevented him from driving big rigs. So he became a limousine driver. How glad we were to have found him.

David hired a personal secretary whose duties included running the official fan club which was getting thousands of letters a week.

An American brunette Corinne Schwab was given the job. She had the highest references of efficiency and was multilingual.

I told Corinne, "Please look after the fans. They're the ones who buy our albums and concert tickets. Give them priority."

Corinne helped share the load.

The team in London had enlarged—executive posts were filled at Mainman by four actors who had been involved with the Andy Warhol play "Pork".

Expecting four actors to fill administrative roles in Mainman was a gamble on Tony and David's part, but it paid off.

All four made an effective transition from their fictional stage roles. They turned out to be quite a quartet: Lee Blackchilders who saved my life in Detroit; Tony Zanetta who became David's personal assistant; Jaime Andrews and the fabulous Cherry Vanilla who had already gained notoriety for writing a marvellously scandalous book of poetry.

Cherry was our Press girl and since glamorisation of a product wasn't new to her she was able to move ahead of us, talking about the whole Bowie legend.

Cherry had so many things going for her. She could talk easily about music because she was also a songwriter, so she made a great travelling companion.

I remember going with her and Tony Zanetta to a place called Springfield in the backwoods of Missouri where a David Bowie Festival was being held.

Unfortunately, David had to remain in London, but we were his delegation for the celebrations at which his music was to be played by other bands on film and on video for the delight of 3,000 of Springfield's young people.

Cherry composed a song, a kind of eulogy to David and his "Space Oddity" creation. It was performed by one of the bands at the festival.

Springfield brought a double celebration for me. My birthday cropped up during the festival. One of David's loyal fans didn't forget. She came along with a beautiful iced cake and hurled it straight at me.

I moved my head and it splattered against the wall right behind me!

We had formed a very special relationship

with America, and the whole way of life that existed there. Especially out on the road.

When it came to the "Station to Station" tour, David was being backed by an eight-piece band and the personnel was thirty-five strong.

Costs were also spiralling. If the music was getting more aesthetic, so was the theatrical concept. The brilliant Jules Fisher designed an incredible set for the "Diamond Dogs" tour which was a replica of a New York street, landscaped to a distant bridge.

Wherever we went this huge set had to be transported with us and erected and taken down after each show.

With all the pressures of the road, at least David managed to preserve his sense of humour. It's hard to behave like a normal human being when you're living out of a suitcase, from hotel to hotel, maybe for three straight months.

In New York I once spent ten hours on a new hair-do. Our hairdresser Suzy Fussey streaked my hair like a rainbow. I vowed that no one was going to miss the importance of David's New York show!

I achieved that much. But changing to go to a party at the Plaza I took a shower and the dye from my hair poured round my feet!

I should have guessed it would happen. I knew it was only vegetable dye and would eventually come out. We hadn't just planned on it coming out that soon.

Suzy, who eventually married Ronno, also took charge of the costumes and wardrobe.

Wherever the band pulled into a town they were confronted by fresh invasions of fans. Everyone made scores of new friends, so when they came home after a tour, I handed out penicillin and told them to see the quack.

I didn't seriously worry about any of David's fans and many of them were very very beautiful.

If I wasn't around and David was hanging out with new friends, I had no reason to feel upset at all.

Rock 'n' roll has some environmental hazards and strangely enough, at the time when this was happening to me, I was not really aware how great a toll the hazards and day-to-day situations make on a relationship of any kind.

How could David play to 20,000 fans who worshipped him and not feel the great love they poured upon him as they chanted for him and the band at the end of every show?

When he was honest enough to say who he had been hanging out with, I was hip enough to accept it as a fact of life.

I also regarded it as a compliment to my femininity to be married to such a desirable and attractive man.

7

*I feel your presence like a pleasure
dream,
My heart's on ffre, my brain could
scream,
There is no joy in silent anguish; only
a bequest
She knew you well, her heart was won
When love reached out and made you
one.
The puppets who danced at her
command
Could never satisfy the girl's demand
No hard, hip, artist; to live in
separation
Was the joy she sought or her dream
sensation.
No rich, indulgent fleeting coupling
Or fame increased by star-fuckers'
suckling.
No pretty boy she could make so rich
And as time marched on, make him
her bitch.
No, for you there had to be a
desperate soul,
A fate eagerly and fatally foretold.
His grasp and cunning were your
titillation*

*No other man could thus ease
frustration,
A heart open wide, so many dwelled
therein
Made of a thousand photographs for
men to spin.
But he alone took time and care
To force at last a love to share
And how he achieved this act sublime
Will someday be counted on the
clocks of time
For his plan, executed with patience'
length
Made love at least win in strategy and
strength.
Is capture of a rare bird cruel?
If you'd dreamed your life as
glamour's fool
There is no orgasm for beauty's queen
Fame buys envy and all things mean
He stole your heart and as you looked
around
Body, soul and face were never to be
found!*

It was a daring, scandalous dress for its day. Two pink satin shells covered my chest and the rest of the creation was formed of strips of pink satin and white printed organza.

Johnny Carson, the celebrated American chat show host, was surprised and the studio producer developed neurotic symptoms.

"That's too revealing," he winced, "you can't wear a dress like that."

I said: "I'm sorry, I haven't got another dress with me. What I've got is what I'm wearing."

Turmoil erupted in the Hollywood studio as they began to bicker. Someone asked: "Who is she?"

"She's down on the call sheet as Jipp Jones," I heard another man whisper back.

"Who the hell is that? What's her claim to fame?" grunted the first man.

"Dunno," replied his companion, "but I've heard she's David Bowie's wife. Maybe that's it . . ."

"Oh yeah?"

I overheard an impresario telling our agent and lawyer Michael Lippman that if I wasn't any good that I would lose David sixty per cent of his audience in the programme that followed, the "Midnight Special".

I had flown all the way from England with the dress folded neatly in my luggage.

Determined at this period to pursue my own career, I had adopted a new name for professional purposes. I was anxious not to trade on the Bowie name, so I adopted the name of Jipp Jones.

David was pleased because I was still using the family name. Secretly he still wanted people to know that I was his wife.

He said, "I want everyone to know that it's my wife they are admiring!"

In London, I had already undertaken a series of modelling assignments as Jipp Jones and I appeared in the national Press with special picture layouts by Terry O'Neill.

In order to get the new name across, all our friends began calling me Jipp but persuading the media to accept me under this identity was an impossible task.

Everyone kept reverting to "Angie Bowie" and on the Johnny Carson Show that was how I was to come through.

David avoided chat shows like the plague. He didn't like them. He was too shy.

"Angie is better at that sort of thing than I am," he would say and RCA Victor saw me as a promotional tool and asset, as did Tony.

"You'll be dynamite on the Carson show, Angie!" cried the RCA executive who looked after our affairs.

But now I was outside the studio sulking in the back of the limousine waiting for the driver to take me back to my hotel, with no show in the offing!

Michael came out to tell me what was going on and to persuade me to go back into the studio.

"They've had second thoughts about the dress," he said, "they think it's going to be okay."

We went back into the studio. Now there was charm everywhere. Obviously the powers-that-be at RCA and NBC had decided that my dress was really neither here nor there and as I was to be offered up as tender bait before David's "Midnight Special", the more revealing the dress the more success I was likely to have.

So now it was all systems go and the countdown to the show started in. . . . I was very, very frightened. I was going on television for the first time!

Among the other guests for the show were Dinah Shore and Joan Rivers and we talked about Princess Anne's wedding. I'll never forget how strange it felt as I nervously sat back while the other guests conducted an almost normal conversation as if sitting in their living rooms at home.

After the show, Mickey Finn, a musician with Tyrannosaurus Rex, who came down to the studio, congratulated me.

"Angie, you did well," he said.

A day or two later I auditioned for the lead in "Wonder Woman", a pilot for the television series.

I guess I should have worn a bra.

When leaping from a wall in my sweater and jeans for a test scene, the director conferred with the floor crew and then asked me if I would mind wearing a bra.

I said I would be happy to do so if they could find one small enough. They did! And we continued.

The "Wonder Woman" role eventually went to Lynda Carter.

Next I was back in New York and asked to do the Mike Douglas Show when it was still being aired from Philadelphia. This time I had to do something very different and as I was already having singing lessons I gathered courage to make my debut. Two musician friends, Mike and Gui Andrisano, were continuing to coach me and they were also instructing me on the arts of choreography.

I also thought that my appearance could be

coupled with a clip from Pennebaker's video film of David's famous "last" concert at Hammersmith Odeon and I went to Pennie's and we edited a suitable extract.

So my appearance was set.

Just before I was about to go on, one of the studio assistants remarked that we were going out live to fourteen million viewers!

"Thanks for building my confidence," I groaned, suddenly feeling a nervous wreck.

I chose to sing an old standard, "I've Got A Crush On You" and I was grateful for the encouragement of the orchestra and its conductor who realised the tension I was feeling.

David was pleased with the way I came across and dedicated another song to me, "The Golden Years." I think it was a coincidence, because he had just finished recording the track about two hours before he saw the California airing of the Mike Douglas Show and he told me the song was for me when he called right after the show to congratulate me. I always felt on top of the world when I got his approval.

I never wanted to use David as a prop, but I always consulted him about my career.

Even before we were married, I was offered a part in a rock 'n' roll movie about groupies. But David advised me against accepting it, as he felt it might be harmful to my ambitions.

Some years later I also rebuffed the offer from London strip king Paul Raymond to pose in the nude for a spread of pictures in his girlie magazine, Club International.

I think Paul had seen a layout of pictures I had done with Terry O'Neill which appeared in The Sun newspaper where I had taken the identities of a saucy French maid, a voluptuous belly dancer and a seductive can-can girl, wearing outfits made by our designer Natasha Korniloff.

They were provocative pictures.

I went to see Paul at his club, where he was standing against the bar.

"I've seen a lot of your pictures," began Paul, "and they're very erotic. Have you got anything against posing in the nude?"

"Yes," I laughed, "a husband!"

The nearest I came to going topless was in an unrehearsed moment on the Russell Harty chat show in England when I was wearing another of Natasha's outfits.

This one was created with a bolero, which accidentally dropped from my shoulders.

"Would you model the gown please?" said Russell.

"Certainly," I replied, "if my tits don't jump out."

The studio audience were in hysterics, Russell hooted with laughter, and the episode was transmitted as it happened, with one censoring "bleep".

In London I worked on a new musical with Lionel Bart. It was called "Carte Blanche" and was to be produced by Ned Sherrin and Michael White.

I adore Lionel. He had ridden the switchback of fame and when he experienced failure, he just bounced back with all his spirit and nerve undaunted.

I think that was as much part of his genius as the successes he had known. He is so unpretentious and a mischievious spirit.

When you're a star and you've got Oscars and gold records and you hang them in the loo—that's lovely. That's where Lionel kept his and he had a huge collection of awards from shows like "Fings Ain't Wot They Used To Be", "Blitz" and "Oliver!"

David despatched all his gold records and awards to his mother and I agreed with him. It's really a mother who should have the pleasure of enjoying the honours paid to their children.

Lionel, with all he had done, should have been rich, but he wasn't. Any money he earned just raced away from him. He was an easy mark always for the spongers of our profession.

He lived in an imposing Chelsea house, the interior of which he designed in the style more reminiscent of a French chateau. There, he would give shelter to all his down and out chums from the East End.

Working with Lionel was a maddening experience, because I didn't always appreciate the intricacies of his genius and if I possessed a grain of a promising idea, I don't think he always recognised it! One night we both got drunk and bellicose and I stormed out from the restaurant where we were dining.

The next morning I was feeling sad and sorry for myself, but our friendship remained unaffected.

Sadder still, our work was wasted. And "Carte Blanche" ran without us!

If my career was moving at all, then there was conspicuously one area in which I was making ground, and that was on the fashion front.

My clothes were as noticed as David's. We were labelled by some as trend setters of the 'seventies, but others had no time for us.

Richard Blackwell, the American designer, took it one step further. He included David's name in his annual list of the world's worst dressed *women.*

David was amused particularly in a year when Disc named him as the world's top international male vocalist.

But our strides into the fashion world made me consider the merchandising prospects.

We negotiated a lucrative contract with Freeman's Mail Order company and Natasha, Freddie and friends spent several months working with us on producing a new eye-catching range of clothes.

Lamentably, on the day we were to sign the Freeman's contract, a clause had been inserted that would have committed David to model the clothes as well as lending his unofficial support to the Freddie Buretti collection.

That was something he wasn't prepared to do and I had made this clear to Freeman's at the outset. Now we were faced with an impasse.

Our hard labours of the preceding months had been lost.

My choice of clothes didn't always please everyone.

Warren Beatty's eye was critical when he took me out for dinner in Hollywood to discuss a supporting role in his upcoming movie, "Shampoo".

He looked incredulous when I arrived wearing a pair of tight pink "pedal pushers", high stiletto heels and a pale green see-through bomber jacket with "Jipp Jones" emblazoned on the back.

I was aware of Warren's reputation as a lady-killer, but I think my outlandish appearance threw him out of gear as he didn't seem to possess the sparkling wit and rapport I expected of him.

Needless to say, I didn't get the part. How much that was to blame on the way I dressed, I shall never know!

I must confess I became increasingly disillusioned by the ambiguities of the film industry. Promises were made without meaning. One project after another bit the dust.

Things looked more promising in Madrid but the movie that was being mounted there ran out of money before the first reel was loaded into the cameras. The movie was written and was going to be produced by Patrick Anderson. It was some story—the premeditated conquest and murder of a covergirl model who unknowingly marries her killer!

In London I was offered the screen role of Ruth Ellis, who at 28, was the last woman to be hanged for murder in Britain after shooting her lover.

It was a very challenging role, but I was confident I could play it. My movie career now looked set to begin.

I was kidding myself.

The screenplay raised objections from the Ellis family and the movie was lost.

Nevertheless, interesting things still happened. I was invited to lecture at Eton College, breeding ground for prime ministers and archbishops. They wanted me to talk to 300 young members of the contemporary arts society.

Their invitation caught the imagination of the newspaper columnists and the headlines said it all: "ETON GOES POP" and "WOWIE —ANGIE BOWIE FOR ETON".

Maybe Eton was trying to shed its prosaic image and I wasn't going to let the reformists down.

While my theme was pretty orthodox—the

105

effects of entertainment on industry—question time turned out to be a ball!

It's a long way from Eton to Las Vegas. There was a song on one of David's albums that executives at RCA Victor thought that Elvis might like to cover . . . the song was "The Golden Years"!

I was so thrilled that I offered to fly to Las Vegas where Elvis was then appearing myself and deliver the tape to him personally.

I hoped to charm him into covering it.

David and I had seen Elvis perform at the Madison Square Gardens in New York some years before. It had been a very special occasion for us, because in those days we were still living in Haddon Hall and to be whisked to New York and given our own suites at the Plaza Hotel was our first taste of star treatment.

Now I was on my way to see Elvis again, proud to think that my husband was signed with the same recording label.

A suite had been reserved for me at the Hilton and I was given one of the best seats in the house for Elvis's show.

Sadly, it was far from being Elvis's greatest appearance.

The show was tailored for Las Vegas, celebrating America the beautiful. A red, white and blue neon set, with the Stars and Stripes flashing, dominated the stage.

Elvis was noticeably overweight and he wasn't enjoying himself because he was conscious of it. He seemed discontented with what he was doing and his selection of songs wasn't balanced. He did a number of versions of "Let Me Be There" and other middle-of-the-road hits.

After the show I went straight back to my suite.

106

Suddenly, I got cold feet about meeting Elvis and the thought of having to lie to him should he have asked what I thought of his show.

It would be impossible to tell him: "Elvis that was just great! Congratulations!"

I'm an awfully bad liar. So I flunked the whole thing, locked the door and went to bed.

Twenty minutes later there was a knock. I went to the door. It was two of Elvis's friends. They invited me for after-the-show drinks.

"I'm sorry," I croaked, putting on a sore throat for their convenience, "but I'm feeling lousy. It must be 'flu. I've had to go to bed. I can hardly stand on my feet."

"That's too bad," said one.

His colleague added: "We hope you feel better in the morning, Mrs. Bowie."

I thanked them.

"Please tell Elvis it was a fine show," I managed to stammer, "certainly very different from New York."

I fetched them the tape and opened the door and gave it to them.

"Now don't forget to give David's best wishes to Elvis and we really hope he likes the song," I said, bidding them goodnight.

I closed the door and leaned back in relief.

Elvis never recorded "The Golden Years" and when he died so tragically three years later I could not help feeling what a fool I was in not having met my idol when all I needed to have done was to button my lip and get dressed up.

8

I've known happiness
I've known sadness
I've met the Mona Lisa
She spelt badness
Some of my best friends are strangers

Another woman came into David's life. And into mine.

Amanda Lear was a divine creature. Blonde and long legged with a sensually husky voice. She was to become Europe's "Disco Queen", now she was the darling of artist Salvidor Dali's set.

When David met her, he set about trying to help her.

Tony signed her to the Mainman label, arranged singing lessons for her and then tried to obtain the movie rights to the Russian cartoon strip heroine Octobriana.

Octobriana—the Iron Curtain's Modesty Blaise—and described as "striding through astonishing adventures, flaunting bare breasts and displaying a spirit of defiance"—was the creation of the Czech defector Peter Sadecky whose book had fired David's imagination.

He could envisage Amanda in the role and said: "She will be sensational."

Amanda lived close to us in Chelsea and she fell in love with David. I imagined they were having an affair, but it didn't seem important enough to bring up.

I didn't discuss it with anybody. I didn't feel it was anybody's business but my own and even now I wonder why I tolerated this ridiculous behaviour from either of them.

But as far as I could see there was nothing I could object to, because I had accepted the role of a dignified and radical thinker on all levels.

Now I was lumbered. How could I suddenly become an impassioned wife screaming abuse about infidelity when I myself had not practised fidelity as part of our marriage vows?

All of this conspired to rob me of my grip on

reality. I tended to become overpowered by my sense of responsibility in terms of duties to perform.

For several months I ran scared over the Atlantic, travelling once a month between London, New York and Los Angeles.

My suitcases were never unpacked. I stayed only long enough for the phone calls to catch up with me. I could not face up to the situations I had been running from.

I would dash off into the night and depart for another destination. I lived high above the clouds in first class passenger aeroplane cabins and it was a dismal life—lonely, unfulfilling and wretched days spent trying to instil a belief in myself that all this activity was leading somewhere, contributing something, and in reality I knew it was to no avail.

David could have affairs with whoever he wanted, I reasoned. But until he started to pay the same amount of attention to me, there was nothing I could do.

Amanda Lear faded from his life. It wasn't that I'd been jealous. It just angered me that David hadn't cared. There were friends in his past who had become dear friends of mine.

Like Dana Gillespie, who had been David's first girl friend.

I laughed, because Dana would tell me, "I was 14 when I first knew David and I was jail bait then."

She was still jail bait. Even at 25. No girl could have flaunted a more amazonian figure than Dana. She was built like Diana the huntress.

Dana had become a very promising star, playing Mary Magdalene in the West End musical Jesus Christ Superstar and a lead in Catch My Soul.

She was making ground both as an actress and a singer. She was also signed to Mainman.

Dana wrote a song, "Weren't Born A Man", which was written for me—inspired by my more gentlemanly qualities, I hope. She had already covered one of David's songs, "Andy Warhol", a musical tribute to the American artist which formed part of an album.

Dana was ready to undertake a provincial tour to plug "Andy Warhol", and she cut off her waistlength hair giving her the look of an untamed lioness.

I was involved with Dana for years and no one symbolised more the meaning of free spirit.

There were spells when David's sexual drive would wane because of the working pressures, particularly when he was writing or meditating over a project.

Then he would say in such moments: "It's not your fault, Angie. I'm not into sex at the moment."

When the pressures eased, his desire returned.

It was a laugh to see him then. He was like a teenager ready to go on the rampage once more.

As you might have gathered our days were never predictable.

I returned home from the airport early one morning, after visiting New York, to discover there were more than horses in the stable!

Daniella was in the kitchen preparing coffee and orange juice and as I put down my suitcases I remarked: "David isn't up, needless to say . . ."

She giggled and she giggled again when I offered to take the breakfast tray upstairs.

I should have guessed from Daniella's reaction that there had to be a reason for her amusement. But it wasn't until I got to the top of the stairs that I was filled with apprehension.

I was about to walk into our bedroom when I wondered if somebody else was in there other than David. So I knocked politely and called out, "Coffee and orange juice" loudly through the louvred bedroom door.

There was no answer so I retreated downstairs.

Moments later a grinning Mick Jagger, along with David, sauntered downstairs together.

"Did you have a safe trip, Ange?" said David.

"Yeah," I said, "what about yours?"

Daniella exploded with laughter.

Our liberated exploits produced many other hilarious moments.

I went out with an exquisite American girl named Janis in Los Angeles. When we made love I kissed her on the neck, catching hold of several strands of her long, golden hair and brushing them back from her slender neck.

As I bent to kiss her again my fingers felt something strange. Suddenly a high pitched whistle echoed round the apartment. At first I thought the alarm system had tripped or the stereo system had been left on.

But the puzzle was solved. My sweet baby was partially deaf and the whistle was in fact a feedback from her hearing aid.

When I related my experience to David, we collapsed in laughter and I wrote a tribute to Janis in the form of a poem. I used poetry to express my feelings about people.

Suddenly we were faced with a conflict of emotions.

I nurtured a relationship with a blond haired musician, whose epicene nature made him all the more fascinating, but I deceived myself into believing that my feelings for him were truly reciprocated. I was just fooling myself. It transpired that he was much more interested in David and had used me to reach him. I felt a dumb, stupid woman who should have realised that from the beginning.

When I was asked to give my definitions about sex to the London Daily Express I told their writer David Wigg: "Sex is a wonderful pastime and if you meet someone who is very good at it and pleases you, then you might go back for seconds or thirds. It might become a habit if it's really that spot on."

My husband was no less candid. He told an American magazine: "I suppose I do fancy blokes quite a bit, but I spend more time with chicks, particularly black chicks. The only type of chicks I can't stand are New York feminists. Get them into bed and after five minutes they want you to do something funny with a light bulb. It's all so academic. And anyway, I love my wife."

You see he always remembered me!

We had created an image, if not a legend about us, and now we had to play the parts.

I don't think it occurred to either of us that ultimately there would be a price to pay for the way we were living.

Our concept of marriage, until now, had run its course but flaws were appearing. Maybe we were just too optimistic that nothing could go wrong, but we had no safeguards.

Suddenly, catastrophe hit me.

I became pregnant.

In any other circumstances I would have

113

rejoiced, but my heart was filled with anguish.

For how could I be certain that the child I had conceived was David's? Could it not be one of the other lovers of our liberation?

I just knew I was pregnant when returning to London after visiting New York. We were coming back on an Australian immigrant liner that was spilling over with passengers, and I became acutely ill. At first I kidded myself it was sea sickness, but by the third morning I knew it was something else—and I knew it wasn't going to be easy when it came to telling David. He always expected me to act responsibly and I thought he would be angry that I had been so undisciplined in taking the Pill.

Contraception had always been my part of the deal, but I had neglected to think about it at the time it must have really mattered.

It took courage to burden David with my anxieties, but his reaction was calm and comforting.

"So that's what it is?" he said, with a faint smile, "well, what do you want to do?"

I sighed.

"There's just a chance, isn't there, that the baby may not be yours," I said, shuddering at the thought.

David's eyes were wistful.

"That's a chance that we will have to take," he replied, "but even so, what difference will it make?"

I embraced David, with tears coming to my eyes. I felt so much love for him. For his patience and understanding.

I thought long and deeply about the situation. I spent agonising hours in conflict with my conscience.

114

I didn't really want to have the baby unless I could be sure that David was rightfully the father.

But I just couldn't work it out. There was too wide an element of doubt.

David indicated that he would leave the decision to me but after prolonged soul-searching I just didn't think I could have the baby.

Supposing it wasn't David's child? Was it fair to him? Or for that matter, was it fair to Zowie either?

There were also other factors to consider.

We had not contemplated having a second child at all.

We had always thought in terms of adoption. I was 23 and at that age the problems and their implications seemed insurmountable.

I became distraught as the chilling, desolate prospect of termination crept into my thoughts.

My mind was transported back to my student days when I shepherded a luckless friend, who had fallen pregnant, to a backstreet operation in Paddington.

At least I would not have to suffer that kind of danger. Attitudes to abortion had move sympathetically with the times and it was now legal in England.

The heartache of such a foreboding decision, however, was not lessened for all of that.

Reluctantly, I made the decision and I was admitted to a private clinic in Hampstead.

While unafraid of the physical aspects, I could not easily come to terms with the emotional aftermath which lingered on long after I had recovered from the operation.

When I was back to normal health, I began to question our life style. I had not lost faith in the initial concept of our marriage, but in the light of my recent experience, I thought it would be wise to make one or two amendments.

And as I told David: "The whole affair has made me question where we are going."

9

"Now my heart beats in time again"

I daresay Hollywood would have approved of David's ingenuity—anyone walking into our living room would find it transformed into a film set.

David used our home as a private film studio, experimenting with video tape and building miniature movie sets resembling Egyptian pyramids, Western-style bars and skyscraper blocks.

Keen to establish himself as an all-round entertainer in the way that Frank Sinatra and Elvis Presley had done, he was simply preparing the ground to break into movies. David believed in environmental conditioning.

Before we were married he had played a minor role as a soldier in the film adaptation of Leslie Thomas's best selling novel "Virgin Soldiers" and he played the lead in "Love You Till Tuesday" for Ken Pitt.

He was now searching for a much more challenging film role and the opportunity came in the Spring of 1975.

Maggie Abbott, a friend of mine who was a London agent, rang me to enthuse over an original screenplay she had just read.

"I think it would be absolutely ideal for David," she said.

The manuscript was delivered to me the same morning. It was entitled "The Man Who Fell To Earth" and the theme was enough to convince me that it would be right for David.

Indeed, it was tailor-made for him. The storyline revolved around the life of an alien from another planet who had come to Earth in the quest for water—the gold standard in his world.

David was in New York and I telephoned him excitedly.

118

"We've seen dozens of scripts. This one is different," I told him, "I think you'll like it." One had to underplay everything to get David the remotest bit interested. But this time his interest was immediately triggered and a few days later, after reading the script himself, he agreed that it was very promising.

Production of the film was already in progress and the young, aspiring British director Nicholas Roeg was signed to direct it. He was interested to think that David enjoyed reading the screenplay.

As cautious as ever, David familiarised himself with Nicholas's previous movies and after acknowledging the sensitive way that Roeg directed Julie Christie in "Don't Look Now" and the way he had interpreted "Walkabout", directing children, David was sure that he could work with him.

In May, the film was underway in New Mexico with locations in Santa Fe and Albuquerque, two romantic names of the old West.

Not only was David the star, but he found places in the movies for his old friends, too. His chum from schooldays, Geoffrey MacCormack, acted as his stand-in. Tony Mascia also got a part, which led to him getting a second role in a Michael Caine film, "The Silver Bears"!

David, of rock 'n' roll superstar fame, plunged into the film game with enthusiasm and aptitude. He was always ready to learn and listen to constructive comments.

Nicholas Roeg was impressed with him.

"What Bowie has is a Garbo quality—the quality of stillness, directly in contrast to what he does on the stage when he sings," he said.

It was a very heavy schedule spanning three months and David found a big ranch that bordered the Rio Grande. It was rugged terrain running into desert and beneath the cloudless sky it was hot and humid.

Luckily, there was a swimming pool and while David filmed, I was able to play and swim with Zowie on days we didn't go to the set. We had a great time together, but our stay there had to be cut short because of the need to get back to London for Zowie's school.

David was sorry to see us leave but I knew there wasn't the slightest possibility of his being lonely or for that matter alone for a second.

The set was full of friends. Some old, some new.

The presence of Sabrina Guinness, who was working on the production, was enough to cause widespread speculation among the gossip columnists.

An interesting feature of this was the way in which people always found it necessary to bring these items to my attention.

I would be lying in bed in the morning, drinking a cup of tea, planning the day with Daniella and the phone would go.

"Hello, this is the 'Daily Dash', we would like your reaction to David's antics in New Mexico with (   )"—at this point one could substitute any name or names.

"Oh," I would say, martyred chastity sneaking into my voice, "isn't it wonderful that David has so many friends in New Mexico to keep him company? Ah, my secretary is with me planning my day, would you permit me to get off the phone?" So I would hang up.

While Sabrina, whose name was once

linked with Prince Charles, was supposedly dangling grapes over David's upstretched mouth, I suspected that his leading lady Candy Clark, an actress from Fort Worth, Texas, was doing the ensnaring.

She had come with Nicholas Roeg to our house in Los Angeles for a script read-through and while I was playing housekeeper and serving wine, she attacked my husband in my own house and was mauling him like a hungry tiger.

Personally, I was shocked and never quite had the same respect for Nicholas Roeg as he had sat and watched the entire episode. He didn't seem to detect my embarrassment.

David looked uncomfortable but tried to take it in good spirit.

Sometime later I noticed in a newspaper interview that Candy boasted how she and David were warned to calm down during the love scenes shot during the film. Nicholas Roeg said they put too much passion into them. How could there be too much passion in any love scene?

If the film wasn't the box office success everyone hoped, at least it was stamped as a cult movie and earned David wide praise.

I think David was at the crossroads of his career: he still wanted to pursue creative things and to write music, but he had long grown disenchanted with concert tours.

In July, 1973 he had suddenly announced his intention to quit before a stunned Hammersmith Odeon audience in London.

As bouquets of flowers were tossed at his feet, David said, "This is my last show ever. There won't be another."

In the Café Royal later that night there was a gala party. It was a truly star-studded night with Barbra Streisand, Elliott Gould, Mick and Bianca Jagger, Ringo Starr, Britt Ekland, Marc Bolan, Dudley Moore, Peter Cook, Lulu and fashion designer Ossie Clark among those paying homage. But how many of them believed it was really goodbye?

David's loyal musicians disbanded to pursue their own careers.

Less than six months later pressure returned David to the concert stage. He had wanted to expand his concert format and I think he used the last show and the threat of retirement into shaking funds out of the powers-that-be. This was one of the few efficient threats an artist could employ. Without an artist's live input, the distribution company—namely the record company—had no way of giving life and spontaneity to their current product.

But the road tours were always harrowing to David and sometimes he lost total control. In Stockholm he proclaimed at a Press conference that Britain would benefit from a fascist leader.

"As I see it, I'm the only alternative for Premier in England," he was quoted as saying.

I knew that David had been working on a film about Goebbels and immersing himself totally into the subject. To make matters even more embarrassing David came into London giving neo-Nazi salutes.

David was living another fantasy soon to be transferred to album and stage performance format. When David found a new identity he lived it totally, until he had experienced everything it had to offer, then he became bored and he would discard it.

Audiences at home in England were

amazed by how they saw him in the BBC Omnibus profile which was titled after one of his songs, "Cracked Actor". David was seen in a loose-fitting suit with braces for the trousers, snazzy socks and a battered trilby perched on the back of his respectable haircut!

One could never predict what David would get into next, but he did develop a penchant for hats and these too would change his entire personality.

Sombreros, Panamas, berets and bowlers . . . David tried them all and we once did a photo session when we wore matador hats in hunting green!

If David was raising question marks about his career, then I was also feeling disturbed by the lack of attention he was now paying to my opinion. In the past it had been customary for us to talk about his career in every aspect.

Now he seemed to rely more on other people whose opinions were usually contrary to mine.

Corinne Schwab, the petite, auburn haired secretary we hired for him, had gravitated to a position of influence.

She was making managerial decisions. She had moved into a supervisory role among the entourage.

Clearly, she was trying to make herself indispensable in David's eyes and she strengthened her position with him by always providing him with an alibi whenever he played truant from home.

She went over the top in Los Angeles and we engaged in a heated exchange when packing David's things for a tour. Corinne threw an empty trunk at me and it smashed against the wall, just a fraction away from me.

I felt it was time I asserted my authority and when we fell out again in Miami, it was time to put Corinne straight.

She made a fuss over some airline bookings I asked her to make and blamed an airport strike for her failure to get the tickets.

Her attitude was hostile, but I wasn't going to listen to any more nonsense from her.

I tossed her through the door of our hotel suite. We were staying at the Fontainbleau.

Corinne was going on to Jamaica with David and the band, while I was returning to London with Zowie and Marion. That mere fact may have been the cause of my agitation.

David always seemed to be going in the other direction and I could not help but think that there were too many periods when we weren't together.

Did I always have to go on sharing his time the way I did?

Loneliness crept over me in London. Marion, Daniella and Zowie were all about the house, but it always seemed empty without David.

I was reminded of his absence whenever I saw his photograph in the newspapers. Sometimes there would be someone else on his arm. Someone fawning over him like a vampire suffocating him.

Seeing enough of these pictures I telephoned him, but couldn't reach him. Corinne came on the phone.

Allowing hysteria to overtake me, I screamed at her, "What is my husband doing? Why is he humiliating me in this way? You get him to the phone immediately. Do you understand?"

The humiliation continued. David began associating with a lot of "drag queens" and again I raged when I saw night club pictures of him in their company.

I'm a Libra and I could find an equilibrium in most things, but I was perplexed by this one.

My supposed best friend David was inaccessible to me both in distance and by his guarded phone. Was he trying to tell me something? Well, he wasn't anxious to say anything or he would speak on the phone. I could find no logic to justify any of the events that were taking place.

I sank deeper into a chasm of gloom. I must have been a terrible burden to my friends. They would pick me up like pieces of broken porcelain and stick me back together again.

I couldn't sleep at nights, yet I didn't want to get out of bed in the mornings to face another day of misery. It was an effort for me to do anything at all.

When I opened my wardrobe and gazed at the clothes, I would feel sick. Because every glittering gown hanging there only brought back memories of our happier days.

The whole thing tormented me and I would slam around the house to stop my memory from plaguing me further.

And on David's return, I would be fine again.

The way I lived seemed parasitic because as soon as I got close to him I inhaled his strength and support.

Because I didn't see him as much as I felt I should have done, I became obsessive about him, although I doubt if I would have diagnosed that at the time.

While I pursued my friends and haunts in London, our world seemed to grow further and further apart.

My apprehension grew in all sorts of areas. Sometimes they were valid, sometimes hallucinatory.

Our close friend Terry O'Neill set up a photo-session between David and Elizabeth Taylor.

There had been talk of David doing "Bluebird" with her in Russia.

Before the photo-session I became very nervous in thinking of David meeting my personal screen favourite and the most beautiful woman in the world.

I guess I had never felt challenged before, not in this dimension.

The photo-session went extremely well, the set of pictures were wonderful. But as I studied them in our home, I gave way to childish suspicion and jealousy.

My rational side counselled: "She is a great actress. There is no way each smile, each look, each nuance of emotion has to have a basis in guilt."

I kept repeating this to myself.

After a totally unfounded event like this my fears would ebb away.

At first I managed to contain apprehensions of this kind but I could not always push them aside.

Our lives were running into strife.

We were no longer communicating in the way of the past.

David was fascinated by black girls and I knew—from the newspapers of course— that he had taken Ava Cherry to Rod Stewart's backstage opening night party in New York.

But now she was moving in with us for a spell prior to the "Diamond Dogs" tour. Ava had been one of David's backing vocalists,

The Astronettes. She was a striking girl with dyed blonde hair.

My attitude to her presence in our home was sympathetic but Ava had obviously never lived in a communal situation and felt she could laze around the house without contributing anything at all except to the pleasure of David, who was hardy ever there. It meant that Daniella and I had to carry her load.

One night I asked her to clear away the dinner plates as Daniella and I were exhausted from preparing and serving the whole meal between two flights of stairs.

She became abusive and I dealt with her sternly.

"The housework has to be shared, madam," I said, and then added, "You always pay for the pleasure . . ."

It was an extraordinary situation. This poor girl had been placed in our house in Oakley Street and as abruptly as she had been uprooted from wherever she had been, abandoned by the person who brought her there—David.

I felt it all quite amazing. My life was getting more like a soap opera.

David escorted The Three Degrees, I think they were in London to do a television show but I remember their single at the time was "Dirty Old Man" and Daniella and I used to sing it all over the house, smirking at which of them was actually David's concubine.

I think David had taken on more than he could handle for to my knowledge all three of the girls had steady boy friends or husbands and I believe there were a few narrow misses in restaurants where unexpected people were dining.

I used to feel like David's maiden aunt indulging a favourite nephew as he regaled me with tales of James Bond-style escapes.

This was all very well except that David disappeared some nights without telling me where he was going or what he was doing. But there was nothing I could do.

In another vein, this was a most delightful period—watching Zowie grow up. My nesting instincts came full circle and as David had planned the original decorations for Haddon Hall I started personalising our Oakley Street house.

I had Zowie's bedroom painted bright yellow, with circus drapery from Harrods and a mural covering one wall which had been executed by a very fine artist, a friend of our builder Mr. Goodchild.

It was a view of the seaside in Cyprus and the sun rising or setting. I loved Zowie's room and it was occupied by the most delightful person. His hair had never been cut until this time (he was nearly five) and hung in long blond curls to his waist.

Zowie would remind me of David's set of chin by the way he held his mouth.

Daniella and I used to sit and watch him playing in the bubble bath. His eyes were a dark violet blue that matched the colour of the porcelain.

He was so beautiful. I still marvel at the work of art one can suddenly, unexpectedly create in a child.

I think this proximity to Zowie had a very bad effect on my judgement and evaluation of the situation between David and myself.

I didn't like causing scenes and somehow, even feeling anguish at David's reported activities, felt stupid in the light of my situation.

128

I had the most gorgeous child, a successful, handsome, talented and ambitious husband. How could I allow myself to become overwhelmed by doubts and suspicions, in fact all the things that our initial marriage vows had warned me of? And so I maintained my composure.

David wanted me to be sophisticated and dignified. I always tried to play that role.

I had to maintain face. For as the doubts gave rise to my own acute anxieties I couldn't allow people to think that everything was not as rosy in the garden of Eden as I had painted it.

It was my business to appear happy and cared for. I was an entertainer.

We couldn't tell anyone that convention was getting its revenge.

I was attending Stevie Wonder's birthday party in New York and for sheer spite I made sure that I was photographed with several friends hoping that David would see at least one of the pictures in the magazines. Maybe he would feel a twinge of jealousy or remorse at seeing me with so many eligible escorts, enjoying myself as I pretended to party through the night.

I was a pathetic little creature trying to justify everything alien to the most common modes of behaviour. No wonder I was having a hard time rationalising it.

We struggled on, but I only suffered more injury to my emotions.

The most disturbing discovery was to learn that David was sleeping with somebody that we had once made love with together.

I felt I had to draw the line somewhere.

I said to David: "Somehow that seems more like cheating, because there is an added

129

insult of me having been left out—that now you return to a situation without me."

I was clutching at straws. Making excuses for David and myself. Fear of losing him stopped me from telling him outright that I could no longer support or deal with this situation. I was no longer able to share him either with black girls, other artists, drag queens or Corinne Schwab: the fantasy had slipped from the frame and was hanging askew.

I could not cope with the uncertainties, the loneliness of my plight.

I met the actor Roy Martin at this time. I had gone to Tramp, the fashionable night club in London. I decided I wasn't going to sit at home a minute longer on my own.

I went out with some other friends. We started having a good time and drank champagne. It was then that I saw Roy for the first time. A gorgeous, dark-haired man in denims who threw a glance at me that made me look straight back at him. His eyes were darkly blue and evil. Eyes I couldn't resist.

I uttered something rude and he made an equally pointed remark back. I laughed and scrawled my telephone number with a ball point pen on the shoulder of his faded Levi jacket.

He was dining with Mick Taylor of the Rolling Stones and Mick's wife, Rose.

He phoned me the next day and we arranged to meet in the evening after his rehearsals for a new play he was going to do.

My parents were in London at the time, staying with us at Oakley Street, and so I left the family at home and sallied forth more excited than usual.

Roy was appearing in the Heathcote Wil-

130

liams play "Remember The Truth Dentist?" He had a leading role.

It was a good play and when one of the actors dropped out of the production owing to rehearsals for a television series in Bristol, Roy managed to get me into the cast.

At last, boards beneath my feet! A chance to work! Interpret someone's lines and give them life.

In my delight and excitement to be acting, I think I must have slipped in love. I did not *fall* in love, for at the same time I knew that there had been no lessening in my devotion and loyalty to David.

Somehow Roy's sense of humour blurred my fears and suspicions as to David's own activities. Perhaps I thought that borrowing a little guilt made us close to the same colour. It was good to have the feeling of a man around once more.

The house sounded different, ringing with laughter again, whenever Roy came to visit us.

I had no qualms about David meeting him. I just knew they would get along.

Indeed, when eventually they got to meet, they formed a firm friendship like two inveterate musicians.

Roy, like David, composed music and he also played guitar, so they had a running rapport from the beginning. And David, far from condemning my relationship with Roy, actually encouraged it.

Maybe I would have liked David to have shown just a trace of jealousy, but he didn't so much as blink an eyelid.

He merely said: "At least I don't have to worry when I'm away now. I know you've got someone to look after you."

Our marriage had entered another extra-ordinary phase.

Roy wrote music and recorded one of my poems called "Soul House". We did promotional shots for the single.

Terry O'Neill, who took the photographs, was into shapes that day. We must have posed in every way together but standing on our heads—but for that matter Roy may have stood on his head.

The results were startling. The theme of Soul House was perfectly personified in this photograph of mingling arms and legs.

The sleeve picture was reproduced everywhere. Everyone seemed to be writing about it.

Danny Secunda, Roy and I went up to Sheffield to continue the promotion in the Midlands. We took Charlotte Vieli who was to be in the Soul House theatre company with us later.

We took a performing mix of the song and went to various clubs and performed the song with Charlotte and myself miming the backing vocals. The Chanter Sisters had sung the originals and Hughie Burns had produced the track.

It was great fun being on the road promoting my first poem to be set to music.

The extraordinary fact of our relationship was Roy's acceptance that I was still in love with David and would go to him whenever I was needed.

David once called when he was in Los Angeles and had 'flu. He asked me to fly out immediately.

I jumped up from bed. Threw some things in a case and asked Roy to drive me to the airport. Which he did.

You could always rely on Roy.

I wonder why I never questioned the motives of somebody who was content to share me with David, or was this the demonic side of my own free spirit beliefs?

I guess it was because I had lived so long cutting off my emotions and pretending that I felt no pain.

I wanted to cut myself off from any sensation which would take the bandage off the raw wound of my emotions.

My emotions and I had been totally incommunicado with each other since the success of "Ziggy Stardust".

10

Money is the sin of Man,
Jealousy and greed of Eden,
Barter and exchange in kind,
were ways of honest men,
Paper, Coin and Credit,
divide us rich and poor,
Our rights no longer equal,
Law and judgement are impure,
Money comes to some,
While millions slave and toil,
Forced struggle culture,
Weeps into the soil,
Nations are exploited,
Freedom is a game,
Puppets are installed,
In Independence name,
Inherit bureacracy and tax,
War and minority conquest,
Economics of obedience,
Invaders on request.

Anger mute,
Of soul and heart,
Will join together,
Make a brand new start,
Sin and evil fight for wealth,
Government controls the land,
Power is their trigger,
So money must be banned.

It was autumn and I had not heard from David for several weeks. Once more the Atlantic divided us.

Our friends, not to mention an inquisitive pack of journalists, were fascinated by the way we managed to sustain a marriage.

Everybody knew I was seeing Roy regularly and they also knew about David's much-chronicled exploits.

Neither of us seemed uptight. In some cases it made them feel prickly.

I was dining in Tramp one night when Mel Bush, who promoted one of David's early concert tours, walked towards me.

His attitude was about as subtle as that of a bull in a china shop.

"Hello Angie," he said "have you seen David lately?"

"What do you mean Mel?" I retorted, my pulse quickening.

"I just saw David in Los Angeles and he looked ill to me," said Mel.

I didn't want to listen to any more of this.

I leapt from my chair and clouted Mel Bush severely.

Rod Stewart and Ronnie Wood, who were sitting at the next table, just seemed to freeze in their seats.

Rod Stewart did his wonderful "I'm looking bored" impression and left me to deal with Mel Bush in whatever way I saw fit. I don't think Ronnie was aware of the incident at all.

Mel must have touched on a sore spot.

I flew to Los Angeles the next morning to make sure David was all right.

He looked great and we hugged at the airport. "Thank God. You look so well!" I exclaimed.

I told him what had happened.

Just a few nights later David and the band were opening their American tour in the Universal Amphitheatre.

There were a lot of celebrities out front in the audience—Diana Ross, President Gerry Ford's family—and Rod Stewart.

When Rod surfaced at the party afterwards, I beckoned him forward and said: "You've met my husband the corpse, haven't you Rod?"

David, that night, was looking terrific.

I wished he could have stayed that way forever, but there was a period some months later when his condition and health warranted genuine alarm.

Whenever David was faced with a new project, he would go into a shell. Invariably he suffered bouts of severe depression, especially when he felt his creative abilities had deserted him.

Every album he cut had to be a commentary on life. He had to be that positive, because he could never allow his critics to hold him to ransom for sitting on the fence.

His last three albums, "Pin Ups", "Diamond Dogs" and "Young Americans" had received wide recognition in the States, but there had to be a sequel and as always, this increased the pressures on David to find one.

For weeks there was silence as he lived with the torment of creating something new and innovative.

From Los Angeles, in the depths of depression, he called me in London.

"Angie," he said, "I don't seem to have anything left to give. I have nothing more to say. I've said it all. What else can I write?"

His voice sounded strangely hollow and morbid.

I tried to give him confidence, to lift him from his melancholy mood.

"There are times when an artist becomes unable to create. As though the resources of experience have been used up. Isn't that what it is David?" I said.

"I know," he said, "but I've got to get something together and I haven't got one idea. That's never happened before. . . ."

I cut in, "But David, it has. You didn't think you could write anything else after 'Space Oddity'. You've had half a dozen albums since then."

David just couldn't grasp what I was saying and when I hung up, I started packing my bags. I had to get to Los Angeles to be with him. This time I knew that he really needed my help.

Arriving there the next day, I was shocked by the sight of David. He didn't look like himself at all.

His face was gaunt, his whole appearance emaciated.

Then I realised the cause. He was staying high too much of the time. He was not using alcohol and drugs as social tools. He was seeking refuge in the loneliness they offered.

David was lost and confused. His path was one of self-destruction, but he was too close to his own reality to see it.

Most people would have sought medical help, but my husband was a loner. It would have been an act of defeat for him not to try and resolve these problems on his own.

David had not managed to write anything new since speaking on the telephone.

"There's just nothing left," he remarked as we drove home from the airport.

Pessimism surrounded David in every

direction. He had severed company with Tony deFries and this was traumatic for him, and now was making his own decisions concerning his career.

Tony had taken on the affairs of other clients, an expansion of the business that David had originally encouraged him to do.

But this occupied the time he would normally have given to David, whose ego demanded all of Tony's attention, which of course, he could no longer give. They had been friends from the beginning, and now their alliance was terminated.

I missed Tony even though I found myself on his wrong side. His original affection for us had long withered. We were no longer the couple of urchins he once said he needed to protect.

Tony's attitudes to us had changed with his awareness of David's financial potential. Money does strange things to people.

My problem was that no one had taught me that the man who handles the money is the one who gives the orders. That, in itself, caused dissension between us.

Quietly, I thought we would survive without Tony.

My first task was to get David looking fit and healthy once more.

I said to David, "Don't worry. We'll get over this crisis, you'll see."

Over the next three weeks my own faith was severely tested as David showed no signs of snapping out of his depression.

Drugs were too easily available in Los Angeles and the environment bred a schedule devoid of normality. I knew David was involved only to escape his torments.

I decided the way to deal with David's

problem was to be patient with him. I didn't want to arouse his anger or suspicion, or to make him appear alone by criticising his activities, so I would indulge to reassure him.

Cocaine would lift the veil on David's depression, but the light that poured in would quickly fade like twilight into darkness. At least cocaine was an acceptable evil.

David was convinced that drugs stimulated his thinking and would come to restore, if not accelerate, his creativity.

But he had not experienced the effects of drugs before. He might have smoked the odd joint.

Frankly, I never regarded marijuana as anything to get too het up about and would have supported any campaign for its legalisation, especially after getting busted myself for smoking a joint in the car on London's Clapham Common! Why I should have had the window down while driving past a bobby I shall never know, but if there was a moral to the story then obviously this was it! The only bad experience I had with cannabis was when I swallowed a spoonful of tincture from what seemed a green medicine bottle and I was laid out flat like an alcoholic.

These minor excursions bore no relation to the situation now facing us in Los Angeles. I knew that someone had to pull David out of it. I'd invite his friends around to see if their company would snap him out of it.

I would sit and talk with him for hours, trying to give him reassurance.

"What has *Charlie* done for you in the last month?" I asked, "what have you written?"

David sifted through some notes and read them over. David pushed the notes from the table. They fell to the carpet in a strewn heap.

"You're right Angie. They don't mean a thing," he said.

He had made an error of judgement. Drugs were not his companion after all and now he realised that.

"I almost blew it all away," sighed David, thankful that he emerged through it with his life intact.

Some months later in a magazine interview he said, "I had more than a platonic relationship with drugs. I was zonked out of my mind. Most of the time I was skeletal. I was destroying my body. I quit because I wanted to go on living!"

That he was able to eliminate drugs by his own conscious deliberation, was enough to fire David's adrenalin once more.

Far from losing his flair to write again, David wrote "Station to Station", which was to become a huge album.

Assured now that David could face the future, I flew back to London.

Our Oakley Street house was haunted by artists and musicians.

Roy naturally hung out there a lot, so too did Dana Gillespie and an Irish actor John Bindon whom she brought to a Christmas party I threw.

We always partied together: Roy, Dana, John and his sidekick Tony Valentine, but Vicki Hodge who was John's girl friend never seemed to be invited, I couldn't understand why. She was a successful English model.

One night we were all sitting talking and I asked them why this was. Before anyone had time to answer I was drawn to the window and shown a red Mini in the street. Apparently Vicki was keeping vigil. I couldn't understand this behaviour and told John to

141

go downstairs and get her and ask her to come in. I had never encountered such a strange situation.

John disappeared out of the front door to talk to her and suddenly there was a crash as milk bottles splattered all over the pavement. We heard shouts and I opened the door and a milk bottle just missed my head.

Every woman should fight for her man, but this was ridiculous. Ducking beneath flying glass, I attempted to convince Vicki to come upstairs and have a drink.

Vicki calmed down and came in. Having met the way we did I guess it was natural that we became good friends.

Her fears that John and I were having an affair were groundless. If I was having an affair with anyone at all then it was Roy and we enjoyed John because of his Irish blarney. He had established himself as a comic by wearing a red dildo taped to his forehead on the night we met.

John and Vicki's relationship was tempestuous and he once tossed *my* mink coat into the Thames in mistake for Vicki's when they were having another of their rows.

I must confess I missed all my London friends when we followed David to New York and gave up our Oakley Street house.

David had found a big house in New York that belonged to an architect. It was situated in the Puerto Rican area and as David said, the whole place had an earthy, realistic atmosphere.

The house suited him perfectly. It was not only spacious but it had an upstairs studio where David was able to instal all his video and taping equipment.

But he was never there, he was always

working or on the road and loneliness began to creep over me. In a house that size, I was like a prisoner in an ivory tower.

David was back to his old tricks.

His film "The Man Who Fell To Earth" was now being premiered in various cities across Europe and he took Bianca Jagger to the opening night in Paris.

Bianca? I remember how we shared a dinner table in Cannes when I had gone to the celebrated French film festival as David's representative to announce his casting in the movie.

It was a magical spectacle and I found myself lunching with stars like Michael Caine and his wife Shakira, John Huston and Michael York.

I had a gorgeous wardrobe of Natasha's dresses for all the ceremonies and I decided my best purpose in being there to promote David's upcoming movie was to keep quiet and to be as charming as possible and so engender a feeling of goodwill towards David.

Now Bianca was at a premiere of this very film with David and I must admit I felt bad about it. Again from newspaper columns, I was told that David went on to stay with Bianca at the Marbella Club owned by Prince Hohenlohe.

I should not have allowed myself to feel in any way jealous because we were long past arguing about one another's indiscretions.

Bianca was a very beautiful and intelligent girl. She was also shy and suspicious of strangers and this made some people believe she was arrogant.

Forgive me, if at that moment, I might have agreed with them.

11

My soul was stretched 'tween love
and ambition
Can opposites ever go to fruition?
My Heart belongs to only one
You showed me life is daily fun.
Work should be studded, crowned
and jewelled
Thus money lust and avarice are
fooled.
I cherish achievement, let it fill my life
Yet such desires cause inner strife,
But now rewards loom close ahead,
Past problems buried, lost and dead.

Golden years have sweetly dawned
Our loyalty and faith the always bond.
Forever at your side
You always as my guide,
Distance is a string
Dimension's mischievous plaything
Slacken it and trust is tested
Tighten it and loyalty is rested.

*Energy or light, all god's recurring
names
Grant us one answer as you play
galactic games,
Tell if our activity which we believe so
right
Is nature's day followed by weary
night,
Or are love and ambition disguising
the true fight?*

Maybe we could still win a reprieve for our doomed marriage, if only we could settle into a home that we could actually call our own.

Clearly, we could never be a family unit while still living virtually out of suitcases.

Every apartment or house we had taken had been rented. I found that to be an extraordinary situation after six years of marriage.

"When will we get a house of our own?" I wondered.

But it was less David's fault than our accountants, who were always worried about our tax position and the delicate procedure of making us residents of any particular territory. Or at any rate, that's what they said.

Ultimately, it was agreed that we should go to live in Switzerland where the tax benefits would be substantial.

I was overjoyed because I thought we would be able to knit our marriage back together and, in thinking of Switzerland, pleasant schoolday recollections flooded back.

I went ahead to arrange residency permits which were extremely difficult to get, but my perseverance was rewarded.

Seven weeks later I was telephoning David to tell him, "We've got them!"

We were going to make a fresh start and we moved into a big cuckoo clock chalet set amid snow-capped mountains.

It was a pity the house was not for sale, because we would have surely bought it. It had lots of room for family life and for any pets Zowie might acquire. The house overlooked Lake Geneva; it was breathtaking.

There could not have been a more peaceful,

tranquil setting. I hoped that it would steady our course. Sadly, it was not to be.

For several weeks I galvanised everyone into getting the house into perfect order. We ordered and hung new curtains; we bought some new furniture which blended well with our other things which arrived from the States and from England.

Eventually everything was in place and the house looked good. I was so proud of it.

But David restlessly paced up and down as though something was wrong. And it was.

"You've worked miracles Angie but I can't relax. It's too much like a postcard," he said.

At first I couldn't understand, but gradually I began to appreciate David's feelings.

My husband, writer of street music, could not identify with the Swiss lifestyle. Not when he was surrounded by it.

David missed his friends and contemporaries in England and America and only when he was able to get away did he seem to be happy.

Our lives fell into a familiar pattern where we tried hard to keep harmony, but things were not helped by the constant aggravation that Corinne caused between us.

She was still asserting her "indispensable" role and she was also acting as a buffer when blocking calls that David didn't feel like accepting for reasons best known to himself.

Once she cut out a call from Ken Glancey, the president of David's recording company, RCA Victor. I asked Corinne why David wasn't taking calls from people who were obviously important to his career. At the time we were spending a week-end at the Chateau de Herouville outside Paris where David was recording a new album.

147

Corinne wouldn't give a me a straight answer and this infuriated me more.

I went and found David.

"David," I said, "you should call Ken Glancey. The man wants to hear from you. No matter how you're feeling at the moment, some responsibilities just have to be carried out. And for that matter it would make everybody's lives a lot easier if you would prevail on Corinne to be more polite on the phone."

At this point, David exploded. He wheeled round and warned me to leave the room. I did.

There was no turning back.

I called a taxi. I picked up my small suitcase I brought for the week-end.

Suddenly I felt giddy. Shock waves ran through my body, like a robot short-circuiting. I clutched my throat, unable to swallow, my eyes began to swell and ran prickly with salt. I thought I was going to collapse.

But somehow I managed to leave the hotel with a modicum of dignity. As the cab sped towards the airport Daniella became scared by my anguished sobs.

"It's all over Daniella, you know that don't you?" I cried. "From this day forth, it's over. . . ."

The days, the weeks slipped by. David went to Berlin. He rented an apartment right in the centre of the city. I was in turmoil, not being able to speak to him face to face, and I couldn't understand why he had gone to Berlin.

He had never asked me if I wanted to live there, but after my first visit to the city my brain cranked into gear.

Corinne liked Berlin.

The penny dropped.

So now Corinne's likes and dislikes were going to dictate the geographical location of my husband and my home.

It never once occurred to David to stay home with Zowie and me.

His boredom threshold was too intense to live with. He swung from genius to the erratic, without warning.

Things were patched up with Ken Glancey who was coming out to Switzerland with his wife to attend the Montreux Jazz Festival and to see David.

David was commuting between Berlin and Montreux as the mood took him.

I arranged a dinner for our guests and Zowie stayed up as a treat.

Daniella, Marion and I worked in the kitchen all day preparing the menu.

Corinne took it upon herself to join us, which was embarrassing because there were only eight place settings. But Marion and Daniella relieved my concern when they discreetly took their meal in the kitchen below.

Frankly, I wondered why a secretary should even have a room in our house. I made it obvious to Corinne that she was no longer welcome.

She got the message. She took her things and moved into a hotel pensione.

The strange thing is that in the beginning I thought that Corinne and I would become great friends. Our lives had passed similar milestones. Like me, she was a European-raised American who had been at school in Switzerland.

I tried to treat her like a sister.

We went shopping together and purchased an entire wardrobe, I bought her presents back from wherever I went, made a fuss of her and the things she was doing, and praised her efficiency.

I honestly thought she would be complimentary to David's entourage.

Usually, first impressions go a long way but in Corinne's case I had cause to think again. Early on, she fell out with David's manager Tony deFries and when he wanted to sack her, I persuaded him to give her another chance.

Corinne betrayed my friendship. She wasn't content to be a secretary. She set her sights on David.

There was no evidence, but I could feel that something was happening. David's demeanour announced it. He was quiet and withdrawn, almost nervous.

"Why do you always get so uptight about Corinne?" he said.

"Because she is in a privileged position and she misuses it," I countered.

Of that, there could be no mistake.

Corinne was exercising a far greater influence on David's life than I was.

She had alienated me from my husband and my position with him had weakened. Why should she enjoy those privileges that were mine as his wife?

Corinne's deception rankled me. Not once was she honest enough to admit that she had more than a platonic relationship with David.

David's infidelity didn't worry me, but Corinne's scheming did. Where was she going to stop?

For David the whole situation and the pressures of his career became too much to bear. He became gloomy. Corinne, whose mother was a psychiatrist, sent him to a shrink!

After one session David came home saying he felt cured.

"You're cured and I'm demented," I raged at him, "You've never had to go to a shrink before. You said you could always work out your own problems."

It was driving me nuts to think that David was only taking Corinne's advice.

"Why not ever ask me?" I thought.

I begged David to fire her. It wasn't the first time that I told him that she was destroying our marriage and that she would have to go, but he always made excuses for her.

"Angie, you don't see all the work she does. You only pick on her faults," said David.

Once David had someone's love and loyalty, he protected them to the end. Besides he hated dismissing anybody.

I thought it would be for my own good if I picked up the threads of my career. I still wanted to be independent.

In London, Dick James, the music publisher who first put the Beatles under contract, wanted me to do an album of my poetry. He was going to pay me a big advance.

I was elated.

Not only was it an incredible offer, but it proved to David that other people believed in my talents and were ready to utilise them.

On the strength of this I bought a white Lincoln Continental car so as to take Zowie back and forth in Lausanne and cut the cost of taxi service.

David was always complaining about the car hire bills and in Switzerland the charges were as steep as the mountains.

Lawyers sent through the Dick James contract to sign and I thought I had just better mention it to David.

But David, instead of sharing my jubilation, remained impassive and said: "Don't sign it. You're signing your life away."

I was astonished.

"It's sixty thousand pounds," I exploded, "that's an awful lot of money."

"What's money?" said David. "What do you need that you haven't already got?"

"Okay, it's my career. Isn't that enough?"

"You'll get another opportunity," he said, "but this isn't the one."

"What do I tell Dick James?" I said.

"Tell him it's the wrong time," shrugged David, "say you've had second thoughts."

I wrote a letter of explanation to Dick. I said to David, "I'm afraid we're stuck with one thing. . . ."

"What's that?" said David innocently.

"The white Lincoln Continental I've ordered to save our taxi bills," I replied, "I thought we would pay for it out of the advance."

"How much is it?" said David.

I told him.

"All right," said David, "I'll pay for it, but it would not have been my choice of car."

David was experiencing a lot of his own contractual and legal hassles at the time. Another managerial dispute led to a parting with Michael Lippman.

Lawyers flew in from the States for meetings with David and were booked at a hotel in Vevey.

Depositions had to be taken the next day, but David mysteriously disappeared.

Finding no trace of him, I summoned Corinne but she pleaded innocence as to David's whereabouts.

Once more, I suspected she was hedging but

152

she wasn't going to blow David's cover however much I swore at her.

This was typical of David. Faced with a crisis, he just went to ground.

As always, I was carrying the can. The lawyers, having flown all that distance, were naturally, upset at the delay.

I just didn't know where to start looking for David. I knew of no one in Switzerland who could have indicated where he was. Then I started calling friends in London, Berlin and further and further away.

I was on the verge of abandoning all hope of his return, when he suddenly appeared at the front door and said: "Okay, I'll see them now."

Luckily, the lawyers had given him just one more day to surface and their vital talks were now able to proceed.

Filled with overwhelming relief by David's return I didn't bother to seek an explanation for his absence. And he didn't volunteer one.

I do not know what was resolved at the meetings but when they were over David said, "From now on I shall be controlling my own destiny."

A more welcome visitor to Switzerland was Roy Martin, who was now more of a friend to David than to me.

David and Roy would go out drinking into the local bars in Vevey and one evening they tottered back, crashing around the house waking everyone with their noise.

I had planned a holiday to Morocco, hoping that I could persuade David to come with me.

But at the last minute he cried off because of a recording session.

"Don't go on your own Angie," he said, "why don't you and Roy go together?"

So we did.

It occurred to me that David might have had a motive for wanting me to disappear with Roy, but who could say.

I enjoyed those three weeks in Morocco!

My next venture with Roy was a business one. Together we formed an experimental theatre group in London, called The Soul House Theatre Company.

Our first show was entitled "Krisis Kabaret" which we staged at the Little Theatre in St. Martin's Lane.

It was a bawdy, satirical revue, our notices were good. David seemed pleased.

Later while visiting him for a week-end in Berlin we got round to talking more seriously about our future. We acknowledged that we could not go on holding our marriage together or making a pretence of things any more.

"You've got your life to live Angie," said David, "and why must we go on causing havoc to one another's emotions? When we married we set ourselves certain rules. Now, if we consider a divorce, then at least we can be civilised about it. We can still be the closest of friends."

It made sense and the way that David framed it, eased any pain I might have felt.

We kissed and shook hands, as if making a bond, and then we went out to tell our friends: "We're having a celebration."

"What for?" they inquired.

"To celebrate our divorce," we said.

David was now working in Berlin where he was producing an album for our friend Iggy Pop, the Detroit rock'n roll singer.

So David and I went out to dinner and I guess we looked more like honeymooners.

154

Holding hands, exchanging affectionate glances, like the couple of urchins we had once been.

Pat Gibbons, who was David's assistant and joined us at dinner, shook his head in disbelief.

"You guys are nuts," he remarked.

Later we phoned more of our friends and cried: "We're getting divorced."

I spent the night with David and when we woke the next morning I told him, "Let's get a divorce more often, darling."

Again, when we split we kissed and were more affectionate than we had been for years. We were going to be very, very sensible.

Yes, we had it all worked out. We were so clever. I went back to London happy in heart, feeling that we had achieved so much.

But the days and the weeks drifted by and nothing happened. I kept thinking how civilised we had promised to be, how this positive approach to divorce might lessen the heartache.

Now we had lost the whole impetus. Earlier I had broken up with Roy and that also caused me pain and sorrow. We had been very close. At one stage I actually fell prey to the stupidity of thinking that I could be in love with two people simultaneously.

You think you are, you swear you are, you're sure it's what it is, but sadly it isn't. It can't be. It's only a safety mechanism you put into play.

I had given what I thought was my love to Roy and he had always been good to me.

When David's money in New York was frozen because of managerial litigation, Roy had supported us at Oakley Street.

Roy had given me the ability to laugh again.

He had also inspired me to work and created new horizons for me.

But when Roy had been drinking it seemed to change his character and I couldn't cope with it.

Out of loyalty, I kept the friendship going long after it should have ended. I felt I owed it to Roy, whose patience had meant so much to me through my own days of ordeal.

I think that both Roy and I knew there was a point where we could not continue our relationship as before and thankfully our parting was amicable.

I wrote another poem for him.

This time a farewell.

12

Silly Satan, you're a clown
never will you make me frown
as you play your silly tricks
words and tunes play with sticks.
As you cast your fiery spells
conjure up your tired old hells
I can tell you plain and straight
all your promises sound too late,
you pretend to make them rich
while their souls are black as pitch
you cannot win while I laugh loud
me and the Lord we is proud
to stamp on your tail, pull off your
horns
jump on your back and avoid your
thorns.
Where I live with those I love
I require the peace of the dove
you are banished as of now
from this moment, out you go,
kerpow!

Our one last chance of a possible reconciliation came in Berlin.

David was suffering, too. He was equally
emotional about our crumbling marriage.

Only days before I arrived to see him, he
had apparently smashed a Mercedes in an
underground car park, trying to do himself
some damage.

When I questioned him about it, he dismissed the episode lightly.

"Forget it," he said, "I was drunk at the
time."

I could see that David wasn't well. His eyes
were red-rimmed with tiredness and his conversation was vague.

I stayed with him in his forties-style Berlin
apartment. There were five or six rooms and
more than enough space.

It was an elegant, old-fashioned apartment
brightened by David's musical instruments
and Zowie's toys in tidy disarray.

Zowie, who was now going to school in
Berlin, was happy there and he had some
friends among the children of his own age.

It must have been on my second day there
that David got us into panic stations. In
the evening he developed sharp pains in
his chest. I telephoned the British Army
clinic and, because they only admitted
military personnel as a rule, I had to be
very persuasive before they sent an
ambulance.

I feared that David was suffering a heart
attack. At the time he was smoking heavily,
as many as four packs a day.

David was given an electro cardiogram that
proved to be negative.

He remained in the clinic for 24 hours for
observation and then he was allowed to

return home. They could not diagnose the cause of his chest pains.

I thought it was a manifestation of depression.

When David recovered, we talked over the ways of getting back together.

"It's something I really want, Angie," said David, "we can make it work, we really can."

I listened to him.

There was nothing more that I wanted than a reconciliation. To start all over again. And to be happy once more and build a home of unity for Zowie to grow up in.

"I would love that more than anything," I whispered, not daring to think that we could possibly manage to find a formula.

It was too much to ask. The one stumbling block would be Corinne.

David wanted me to go to Berlin to live with him, but I told him I wouldn't consider it if Corinne was going to remain there as his secretary.

"If Corinne goes, then I will think about it," I said.

"Angie, how can you ask that?" protested David, like a schoolboy, "you know how much I rely on her. She's part of the organisation. She knows everything about my business. Who else could run it the way she does?"

"I could," I said.

He made no reply.

"That's it. How can we seriously talk about a reconciliation if you want to hang on to the things of the past?"

I strongly resented Corinne's presence in the house, particularly during my visit.

It was impossible even to think about a solution, knowing that she was always hovering in the background.

Things were never going to change.

David went out one night and did not return. Corinne provided an alibi for him.

"Why do you go on lying to me?" I screamed at her, "Why can't you tell the truth, just for once?"

We had a most terrible row. She stormed out. No longer responsible for my actions, I went into her bedroom and threw open the wardrobes. Amid tears I seized every dress, coat and garment I had given her over the last six years and I dumped them in a pile in the centre of the room.

I grabbed a bottle of vodka from somewhere and poured it over them and then I struck a match, attempting to set fire to them.

Thank God, I couldn't get them to light and the clothes were left piled in a soggy heap.

I must have taken leave of my senses.

Corinne had driven me to behave like an animal, terrified as hunters move in for the kill.

In despair, I left for London.

I heard no further word from David until he invited Zowie and me to spend Christmas with him in Switzerland.

Believing that families should be together at that time of the year, I agreed. But I was in for a nasty shock. Suddenly, plans were changed and I wasn't told until my arrival in Switzerland.

David intended transferring the quiet Christmas at home to a social knees-up in Berlin, where he was then involved in filming "Just a Gigolo" with Marlene Dietrich and Kim Novak.

I might have gone along with the idea, until

I learned that Corinne would be staying with us in Berlin.

It was the last straw!

Ensuring that Zowie would be safely looked after on the trip to Berlin by Marion and Daniella, I fled on the first plane out of Geneva.

Its destination was New York and I took it. After eight hours in the air, I was still seething when the plane landed. It then struck me that I had nowhere to go.

I rang one of our tour friends, Keeth Paul, the first person I could think of contacting.

Keeth, a sound engineer with The Heartbreakers, was spending Christmas with his mother, but detecting my anguish, he said,

"Come and stay with us. You can't be alone in New York over Christmas. Are you crazy?"

I didn't want to burden Keeth's mother with my troubles, but she was very kind and didn't regard me as an intrusion on their celebrations.

Over the holiday, I developed a close affection for Keeth because of the concern he showed for me and when I thought about going back to Switzerland he insisted on coming with me.

It was January 2 and when we got to Switzerland the house was empty. Zowie and Marion were still in Berlin but the story broke in the newspapers a day or two later that David had snatched our child from me because I had selfishly abandoned him! This was hardly the case.

I was frantic. I may not have been a full-time mother but I always cared for Zowie and at all times he was uppermost in my priorities.

This accusation was a slur on my character.

I wanted to get even with David, but I didn't know how.

I had run out of money and I wasn't going to call him to ask for any.

I telephoned David Lewin, an English journalist in London, and told him I was ready to give my side of the story.

"But I've got to have some money," I said forlornly, "I haven't got a bean."

Lewin contacted one of the Sunday newspapers. I got a call from the London Sunday Mirror Editor. He promised to send over some cash with a reporter and photographer.

When I put down the receiver, I freaked out. What on earth was I doing? It was like pawning my soul.

I was beside myself and went up to the bathroom and emptied a bottle of sleeping pills into my hand. I swallowed them with a glass of water.

The house was so big, but it began to encroach on me. I began smashing up things. I didn't know where Keeth was: he might have been out in the grounds.

I was no longer capable of knowing what I was doing. I ran through to the kitchen and attempted to stab myself with a steel carving knife, but I dropped the knife from my hands.

I was on the stairs once more and reeling. My head was swirling. The pills had taken their effect and I plunged down the staircase.

When I became conscious I was in hospital with a doctor leaning over me, his face wearing an anxious frown.

"You're a very lucky young lady. You could have died," he said.

I left hospital two days later with Keeth and 'Sunday Mirror' reporter Tony Robinson, who was to hear of the torment I had come through.

"My husband branded me as a negligent mother. How could he?" I sobbed, my face battered and bruised from my fall down the staircase. I had also broken my nose.

As soon as I could travel I flew to New York with Keeth and we took an apartment off Broadway. My nervous system was shattered and only a few days after we arrived I found myself alone once more because Keeth had to go out on the road doing gigs with his band.

My despondency worsened. Again I thought about suicide. There didn't seem anything to live for. What was the point of going on?

Once more I poured a bottle of sleeping pills into my hand and I had just popped the last one in my mouth when the doorbell rang.

It was an 18-year-old boy who was one of a bunch of friends I had met with Keeth. He knew I was alone and he was on his way to a party.

"Why don't you come Angie?" he said.

I was flummoxed.

"I don't know," I said, my head already spinning, "first let me take a bath, then I'll see."

I thought a bath might revive me and counter the effect of the pills.

Leaving the kid in the living room with a pile of magazines, I went to the bathroom, ran the water and locked myself in.

I got undressed and now I was reeling. I must have collapsed as I actually climbed into the bath.

The poor kid waited for me but was too embarrassed to disturb me until he realised that something was wrong. When he called and knocked on the door to find there was no answer, he broke in and found me slumped in the tub.

He rang for an ambulance.

Again, I was on a stretcher heading towards hospital where I was given a stomach pump. It was a nauseating experience and one that I will never forget.

The one consolation that came was that it cured any other suicidal tendencies I might have entertained. I couldn't go through that again.

When I looked back on it, I felt nothing but degradation and disgust to think that I had even contemplated taking my own life.

It was some time before I regained my sanity and dignity and when I did, I had to condition myself to the fact that David was finally pushing ahead with a divorce.

But his lawyers made it clear that it wasn't going to be on the amicable treaty that David and I had once thrashed out in Berlin.

Now they were accusing me of being a negligent wife and mother and these accusations constituted the grounds of David's divorce writ.

Poor Marion and Daniella were hauled in to swear affadavits on David's behalf, testifying my absence over Christmas and how I had left Zowie with them.

I saw Marion in the summer. She cried in my arms and told me that she never wanted to be disloyal to me but she'd had to tell the truth.

I said, "I understand Marion, don't fret. All I hope is that you didn't invent anything."

Marion shook her head.

"No of course not," she said.

But she then bit her lip and said, "I don't

164

know if they got the whole truth, because they only asked me about this one incident."

My standards were questioned by the lawyers.

In England there's a saying that people in glasshouses shouldn't throw stones.

Let them question David's standards before challenging mine.

In Berlin David had been having an affair with the German night club drag artiste Romy Haag. They had met while she was starring as a female impersonator.

Romy, who was described as tall and beautiful and having the "looks of Sophia Loren", decided to tell the London Daily Mirror all about her romance.

She said: "To know the real David Bowie you can't do anything but love him. The saddest thing in my life is that our beautiful relationship as lovers is over.

"I have never considered myself to be a man, neither did David. God, how I love him."

Romy also said: "Angie seemed to accept our relationship."

Accept? By that time I didn't care. David had humiliated me enough.

13

Thus, ideas logically cannot be owned: they are the property of the universal mind—the Energy of the Earth.

The moment that caused me the most anguish in the pending divorce with David was bringing myself to tell Zowie. But now that he was nine, I figured he was old enough to know the truth about the situation that existed between his parents.

It was going to be hard for him, but I resolved it was far wiser to be honest with him before he was asked awkward questions.

I didn't want Zowie to live in any kind of shadow.

Zowie had started his school life in a kindergarten in London, he had also gone to school in New York and Berlin, and now he was happily immersed in his new surroundings in Switzerland, where we hoped his education would not suffer further interruption.

Zowie was very bright and showed a natural gift for learning and listening. Like his father he possessed a keen, alert mind and he could pursue and establish three or four different interests simultaneously.

I was optimistic about his school career, although having acquired a children's professional drum kit from one of David's musician friends, I suspected that he might follow in his father's footsteps!

Blue eyed and as lithe as a dancer, Zowie looked so much like his father. I once saw one of David's photographs as a boy and compared it with one of Zowie's at a similar age. The resemblance between them was striking.

Zowie loved us both so much and despite what I felt about David I never criticised him. He had always been a fantastic and model father, inspired by the deep love David felt for his own father.

David cared about children.

When in September 1977, our friend Marc

Bolan was killed in a car crash, one of the first things that David did was to set up a trust fund for his infant son Rolan.

To see David conducting a children's programme was magical. He would have no problem in persuading the youngsters to sing or to play any sort of instrument. He was always marvellous with them.

As a mother, I also tried to show Zowie that same kind of understanding and patience. He was a very sensitive boy and I remember, how as a toddler, he sprawled on my bed when I was sick in London and held my hand, the tenderness running from his little heart.

If he grew up bearing these qualities of honesty, compassion and understanding, then I could not ask for anything more.

I was naturally protective of him and if he ever had a problem we would solve it together.

Telling him about our intended divorce was a task that may have caused me more pain than Zowie. For children are much more sensible about these matters than we parents imagine.

David thought that Zowie already guessed, but I considered he was slightly bewildered by our uncompromising attitudes to one another.

So I tried, as gently as possible, to explain to Zowie that although I still loved his father, and his father loved me, we just couldn't live together all of the time because we could not always agree on certain things.

I said that over the years we had changed, like all people did and we now held different views from the ones we shared when we were married.

But I told Zowie: "Don't fret about it,

because we will always be good friends. And when we talk to one another, we're always happy because we always talk about you! You are our great joy."

Zowie nodded. That inquisitive face of his yielded such wisdom and understanding for a child of his age.

A few weeks later I flew into Switzerland to see him and he was in fine shape. He was excited to see me and he had come to terms with the situation that existed between David and me.

Deep down he knew that he could still see us both whenever he wanted to, so he had not lost that vital sense of security that a child must have.

I did not stay at the house. I checked into a hotel in Lausanne and Marion brought Zowie over during the daytime.

I took him out on the lake for boat trips, we made special outings to Montreux and together we spent four idyllic days doing all the things I knew he enjoyed.

In the meantime, I had to meet David and his lawyers about finalising the details of our divorce and the thorniest part was the terms of the settlement.

There were too may clauses advanced by David's lawyers that I could not concede. I was to be given a house and alimony and at first it all seemed perfectly acceptable but then I thought more carefully about it.

I was only 28. Supposing I did marry again and have more children? Under one of the clauses I might lose the house and while Zowie was protected, if I had any more children there would a risk of them becoming second-class citizens.

It was a remote danger, but one that I could

not remove from my anxieties in agreeing to these settlement terms.

The other galling prospect was that because the divorce was being executed under Swiss law, David, as a resident, was entitled to the custody of Zowie and I would only be offered "reasonable access".

My argument that a mother was as qualified as a rich and respected entertainer to bring up a child went unheeded.

So I decided to fight the settlement terms and this led to protracted negotiations.

What grieved me greatly were David's accusations that I was a negligent and unfit mother. I could not conceive how my husband could have said such a thing. He knew how much I loved Zowie.

His accusations ran like a blade through my heart. For days I did not eat or sleep, just wondering why David should nurse such malice.

David could always be hard and cold in defending issues that were close to him but it was a stance he took only in business matters, not when it came to family affairs.

Yet I knew how much he had changed. He was now cynical, private and secretive. And he had never been any of those things before.

Eventually, after two years of squabbling, we managed to reach agreement but it took a long time before the heartache got anywhere near to being healed.

When I last saw David we had coffee together in Lausanne. We were like two strangers and I left wondering: "Was this the man I married?"

14

Without the Blood I am alone,
The Blood is my soul and bone,
The Blood he knows just what to do,
The Blood he do what I like,
Without the Blood I am through.

David once said, "How could I ever let go of this divine being?"

I thought about those words as we entered the throes of divorce.

I was sad that a marriage, a way of life, the things I wanted for my husband and had worked so hard to attain for him, to see him flourish and develop as an artist, should disintegrate in the corridors of superstardom.

I was sad that we failed to make our concept of marriage succeed. That will be the one regret of my old age. We came so very, very close to it.

The experiment was valid. But unless you have honesty and total communication with one another, you lose your ideals.

We fell victims to our own philosophies.

Infidelity wasn't the killer. When I try to analyse it now, I can only regret the amount of time we spent away from each other.

It's not humanly possible to stay in touch with a person and to show them that you care, when you don't spend any time with them.

I think that infidelity preys on your mind during long days of absence, so it becomes important when it didn't have any meaning before.

I endeavoured to act ethically. But I hurt myself most of all.

My mistake was in not telling David that I would have preferred to live another way, yes, even as a conventional wife, if it would have saved out marriage!

I should have said more, but he always looked so bored. I hated trying to talk to someone who looked bored.

Maybe, on the last run in, we should have

made our home, not in Switzerland, but in Cyprus, because he shared my empathy with the country. Maybe that's where we could have repaired all the damage that our marriage had suffered.

Our friends were comforting. They didn't take sides, but they rallied round in the final hour when just the mention of David's name would cause me to collapse in tears.

Today, I feel differently.

I'm trying to shed the identity of Mrs. Bowie because I feel it doesn't rightfully belong to me any more.

I've also learned something about sex. Once I just regarded it as a physical thing and unimportant. Now I know it is something very precious that can only be shared with the one person you love.

I've met someone like that. Isn't it a gas when you do? Kind of a crazy guy, devoted to the truth and making life uncomfortable for hypocrites.

Looks mean, or looks keen.

He was born in Cheshire of Polish descent, a songwriter and performer but dedicated to being a free spirit above all.

I met Drew—or Drew Blood to those of us who know him in London.

From the depths of despondency his discipline and cautious logic beckoned me. I was living on my nerves and drugs, doing anything that took away my ability to whip myself a little more. Having failed in the great project of my life, I made it all seem so dramatic, as if I had been deprived of my very birth right. What a self-centred creature!

Drew had no time for any of it and was amazed that I wasted an ounce of energy on anxiety or recrimination.

The fate of all human beings rests on love. That is the trick to transfer personal emotions, so they spill over and influence how we feel about all people. The more love there is to spread around, the less unhappiness and violence is engendered. This must be the ultimate aim of all artists, politicians, soldiers or clergy—to spread as much love as they dare in the course of a lifetime.

EPILOGUE

*I am so far from landmarks touched
and cherished
an exiled lover of all that England is
a million soldiers and writers
perished
to keep that land, they said, as 'tis.*

*Did no one tell our wasted youth
tomorrow's aims are not their own
who warned them of the twisted truth
which politicians and the greedy loan
to some group called electorate at
interest rates so high
they rish their power every day, but
people do not always buy.*

*How to compare a land fair as
heaven,
sweet as paradise with talent and
intellect.*

*Electorate is surely people, even as
you and I
If you now had to leave your home,
wouldn't you rather die?
I am sad so deep inside myself,
the shock of this straight fact
does not really connect at all,
my heart and I have made a pact.*

*I shall not cry for what's gone before,
I shall not swear or curse
but every day I'm away from home
I shall always be the first
to rave about my beautiful land
our clever intellectuals our brilliant
industrialists
the entertainers that entertain the
world.*